SOLDIER H: SAS

THE HEADHUNTERS OF BORNEO

D1589926

SOLDIER H: SAS

THE HEADHUNTERS OF BORNEO

Shaun Clarke

First published in Great Britain 1994
22 Books, 3 Sheldon Way, Larkfield, Maidstone, Kent

Copyright © 1994 by 22 Books

The moral right of the author has been asserted

A CIP catalogue record for this book is available from the
British Library

ISBN 1 898125 09 0

10 9 8 7 6 5 4 3 2 1

Typeset by Hewer Text Composition Services, Edinburgh
Printed in Great Britain by Cox and Wyman Limited, Reading

Prelude

The landscape consisted of dense, often impenetrable jungle, swamps, rivers so broad and deep that they were frequently impassable and aerial walkways created at dizzying heights over the rapids by the primitive tribesmen. Snakes, scorpions, lizards, poisonous spiders and dangerous wild pigs infested the whole area. Though seemingly uninhabitable, the jungle was home to many native settlements, or kampongs, most located either by the river or on a hillside, where the inhabitants tilled the land around them or hunted for fish, lizard, boar, deer, baboon, porcupine or the ever-present snake.

These primitive peoples were Land Dyaks, Ibans, Muruts and Punans, who lived in longhouses made of atap wood, with sloping roofs of tin or thatch. The longhouses were apt to creak balefully on the stilts that had kept them out of the water for decades. Inside they were unhygienic and usually fetid because as many as fifteen families would live in a single dwelling at any given time, using the slatted floor as a communal lavatory. Small and indolent, the natives wore nothing above the waist, regardless of sex, wore their hair long, often tattooed themselves against evil spirits, and lived off rice, tapioca, vegetables and curried meat. Before being killed for eating, their prey was first stunned by a virulent nerve poison borne by on a slim bamboo dart shot from a blowpipe.

Early morning in the jungle and swamps was often misty. The strong sun did not break through until at least mid-morning and most afternoons brought a torrential deluge of rain, accompanied by spectacular electrical storms. As a result, the water often rose 30 feet in a single day, slopping and splashing around the stilts of the longhouses, making them groan in protest.

Because certain of the tribesmen, notably the headhunters among them, thought the creaking and groaning were the whispering of bad spirits, they attempted to keep the spirits at bay by stringing up shrunken human heads on the doorposts atop the entrance stairways.

Many of the primitive Iban tribesmen, being experts in jungle tracking, had been employed by the British during the Malayan Emergency of 1948–60 as Army trackers, and were dubbed the Sarawak Rangers. Now, in 1963, having been trained by the SAS, they had been recruited again as an irregular force, the Border Scouts, used mainly as trackers, but also armed and trained as paramilitaries. Increasingly under the command of, and working alongside, the Gurkha Rifles, they were engaged in the 'secret' war being waged to protect Sarawak, Borneo, from the forces of Indonesia's ambitious President Sukarno, who were striking from neighbouring Kalimantan.

Enlisting the aid of the indigenous population, and with the additional reconnaissance and intelligence support of the men of A Squadron, SAS, the Gurkha-led patrols made cross-border raids against the Indonesians, worked at winning the hearts and minds of the jungle dwellers, and set up many Scout posts and observation posts (OPs) in the kampongs and along the densely overhung river banks.

At Long Jawi in Sarawak, 30 miles from the border with Kalimantan, the Gurkhas had established a Scout post consisting of twenty-one trained locals, or Border Scouts, two Police Field Force signallers and a six-man Gurkha team headed by SAS corporal, Ralph Sanderson, on loan to A Squadron from D Squadron. Operating from their own riverside longhouse just outside the village, the members of the border team had spent weeks making friends with the tribesmen in the other longhouses in the area, training certain of them to be armed Border Scouts, and patrolling the valleys, not only for intelligence about Indonesian Army or CCO – Clandestine Communist Organization – troop movements, but also to map out a possible route across the jungle-covered mountains between Sarawak and Kalimantan.

Nominally in charge of such missions, Corporal Sanderson had immersed himself in local culture to such an extent that he was treated by the natives as one of their own and was told all they knew about Indonesian activities in the valley and across the hills, where the build-up of uniformed enemy forces was increasing daily.

Though the SAS were not yet under orders to take aggressive action against such forces, they were allowed to embark on reconnaissance and intelligence-gathering (R & I) missions and, if they sighted the enemy, to inform the Gurkhas and guide them and the armed Border Scouts back across the border. The Gurkhas and Border Scouts would then attack the enemy and make a subsequent hasty retreat back to the Scout post on their own side of the border.

These experiences had filled Sanderson with admiration for the skill and courage of the Gurkhas, but left him with mixed feelings about the Border Scouts. Although fond of the tribesmen, who were superb as trackers and good-natured as comrades, he was convinced that training them as paramilitaries was a waste of time. As well as lacking any sense of discipline, they simply could not learn to handle their weapons properly, and were always pointing them accidentally at one another when they were cocked and loaded. It was the corporal's belief, therefore, that while the Border Scouts were dependable as trackers, they could not be relied on in a fire-fight and might even be a liability.

Sanderson did not know it, but he was about to be proven right in a most forceful manner.

Just before dawn one day in September 1963 a well-equipped company of Indonesian regulars made an attack by river on Long Jawi, emerging from the early morning mist. The Border Scouts manning the GPMG (general-purpose machine-gun) in a protective sangar at the edge of the river, just outside the Security Forces longhouse and the kampong 500 yards east of it, had been drinking *tapai*, a potent local cider, the night before and were sleeping soundly at their gun when the Indonesian boats slid into the river bank. The Border Scouts were still sleeping it off when the enemy troops, all wearing jungle-green fatigues and carrying Armalite M16 5.56mm and Kalashnikov AK47 7.62mm assault rifles, slipped off the boats, spread out in a broad firing arc and advanced quietly on the longhouse. While they were doing so, more troops disembarked behind them to set up two 7.62mm RPK light machine-guns spaced so as to cover both lines of retreat from the longhouse.

The first of the Border Scouts was awakened by the snapping of twigs on the jungle floor as the Indonesian troops stealthily approached his sangar. Looking up and seeing two of them practically on top of him, he managed to let out a shrill cry of warning before the enemy guns burst into action with a deafening roar and a combined hail of 5.56mm and 7.62mm bullets tore the sangar apart, turning the Scout into a convulsing rag doll of torn clothing, punctured flesh, exposed bone and pouring blood. The guard next to him suffered a similar fate before even lifting his head, expiring in an explosion of swirling thatch, bamboo and dust from the exploding walls of the devastated sangar.

The Security Forces men also inside the longhouse were rudely awakened by the roaring of the guns outside. First out of his hammock was Corporal Sanderson, who almost in one movement rolled off the bed and landed on his feet on the slatted floor. Picking up his self-loading rifle, he rushed to the veranda while the two Police Field Force signallers and a six-man Gurkha team sharing the longhouse were still struggling to get their wits together. Running at the crouch out through the entrance and along the veranda raised high above the ground, he saw that the Border Scouts who had been sleeping around the longhouse were perishing in a hail of bullets from the Indonesian raiders. The latter were spread out across the clearing between the river and the longhouse and firing their weapons on the move.

The combined roaring of the two Indonesian RPK light machine-guns, fired simultaneously to spray the front of the longhouse, filling the air with flying splinters of bamboo and thatch, merely added to the general bedlam of gunfire, ricocheting bullets, shouting and screaming.

Realizing instantly that there was no hope of defending the longhouse, Sanderson fired a couple of bursts from his SLR. He had the satisfaction of seeing a couple of enemy troops fall down, then he bolted around the corner of the longhouse – the veranda ran right around it – as some Gurkhas emerged from inside, bravely firing their SLRs from the hip. More Indonesians were cut down, but the Gurkhas were punched back by a fusillade of enemy gunfire and collapsed with pieces of clothing and bloody flesh flying from their torn bodies. Even as they were dying, their killers were racing up the steps of the longhouse, still firing on the move.

Now at the side of the longhouse, Sanderson saw one of the two Police Field Force signallers frantically working the radio on the communal table while the other shouted instructions in his ear and the remaining Gurkhas fired their weapons at the entrance. In a futile gesture of defiance, he aimed his SLR through the window-shaped opening in the wall and opened fire as the Gurkhas were cut down by a hail of enemy bullets and the first of the Indonesians burst into the room. The slaughtered Gurkhas were still being bowled backwards by the bullets, knocking chairs and tables over, as the Indonesians shot by Sanderson quivered and collapsed. Those behind them, however, either opened fire on the hapless signallers – blowing the radio to bits and turning one of the signallers into a shuddering quiltwork of shredded cloth and spurting blood – or turned towards Sanderson, trying to locate the source of his gunfire.

The second signaller was still tapping the Morse code keys frantically when a *parang* swept down through striations of sunlight and sliced off his hand. Before he had time to feel the pain and scream, he was shot through the head with a pistol. The man who had shot him was in turn dispatched by a burst from Sanderson, before the SAS corporal turned away from the window – the other Indonesians too were now aiming at him –

8

and vaulted over the bamboo wall of the veranda as bullets whistled past his head.

A former paratrooper, Sanderson landed on his feet, let his legs buckle, rolled over a few times and jumped back up as a group of Indonesians, one carrying a flaming torch, raced around the corner of the longhouse. A short burst from Sanderson's SLR bowled over a couple of them, including the one carrying the flaming torch. Falling, the man set fire to himself and started screaming dementedly, his feet frantically kicking up loose soil as some of his comrades tried to put out the blaze.

Meanwhile Sanderson had slipped into the jungle and crept around the back of the longhouse, carefully covering his tracks, while the Indonesians who had seen him plunged on ahead without checking, assuming he would flee in a straight line. As they disappeared into the undergrowth, Sanderson kept circling around the back of the building and saw, through the dense undergrowth, that the Indonesians were setting fire to it. Moving further away, still concealing his own tracks and footprints, he headed for the kampong, to where the sounds of shooting and screaming had spread. Through a window in the undergrowth he saw the Indonesians throwing blazing torches onto the verandas of the simple houses while the natives, men, women and children, fled into the jungle.

Having seen enough, and aware that there would be no survivors in the longhouse, Sanderson turned away and headed deeper into the jungle.

When he glanced back for the last time, he saw, through the narrowing window in the undergrowth, that the raiders were looting the kampong and destroying it by fire. When they were finished, he knew only too well, they would withdraw in their boats, leaving nothing but smouldering ruins. As there was nothing he could do to prevent it, Sanderson looked back no more.

He moved at the crouch deeper into the jungle, weaving broadly between the trees, stopping every few minutes to concentrate on the silence and allow any enemy troops in the vicinity to give themselves away by their movement. As he had anticipated, the group pursuing him had broken up to fan out, hoping to find him sooner that way.

One of them materialized straight ahead, his presence made known only by the slight shifting of foliage. Not wishing to give his presence away by firing his SLR, and also in need of rations for what he knew would be a long hike, Sanderson very carefully lowered his SLR to the jungle floor, unsheathed his Fairburn-Sykes commando knife, and inched forward to the shifting, whispering foliage. Rising up silently behind where the foliage was moving, he saw the shoulders and back of

10

the head of the enemy soldier in jungle-green fatigues.

Sanderson stepped forward without hesitation, letting the bushes part noisily, to cover the soldier's mouth with one hand, jerk his head back and slash across his throat with the knife, slitting the jugular. As the man went into a spasm and his throat gushed warm blood, Sanderson kept his mouth covered and held him even tighter, ensuring that his convulsions did not make too much noise. The dying soldier struggled very briefly, choking on his own blood, and eventually went limp in Sanderson's arms.

Lowering the dead man gently, almost tenderly to the ground, though this was solely to keep the noise down, Sanderson removed the webbed belt containing his victim's survival rations and placed the belt around his own body. Then, after going back to pick up his SLR, he headed carefully into the jungle once more.

Four days later, after an epic journey through jungle and swamp, across rivers, through uncharted valleys and over densely wooded hills, using nearly invisible tracks and dangerously swaying aerial walkways, braving snakes, scorpions, wild pigs, charging boar and headhunters, Sanderson – slashed by thorns and palm leaves, bitten by mosquitoes, drained of blood by leeches, a stone lighter and almost starving, his uniform in tatters and his feet badly blistered – stumbled out of the jungle in the early-morning mist of Kuching, Sarawak, and staggered up to the guarded main gates of SAS HQ.

'I have something to report,' he croaked to the astounded trooper on duty. Then he collapsed.

1

The briefing took place in the new SAS head-quarters, a large house lent to them by the Sultan of Brunei and known as the 'Haunted House' because during the days of the Japanese occupation, when it had been used as an interrogation centre, a young British woman had been tortured to death there and was now said to haunt the place. Even so, it was a great improvement on the makeshift headquarters the SAS Squadrons had been using previously, containing as it did a communications centre (COMMCEN), sleeping quarters, showers, recreation room, and other rooms such as the lecture hall where the briefing was given.

Leading the session was the Squadron Commander, Major Patrick 'Paddy' Callaghan, who felt completely at home in Borneo after having served his stint in Malaya during the Emergency. Also, though many SAS officers felt ill at ease when first confronting their notoriously critical troopers

– it was the SAS NCOs, after all, who picked
the officers during Initial Selection and thereafter
judged them sternly – Callaghan felt comfortable
because of his lengthy experience with the SAS since
its inception in World War Two.

In fact, Callaghan had been one of the very
first officers to work with the regiment's founder,
Captain David Stirling, alongside the Long Range
Desert Group in North Africa. After a few years
back with his original regiment, 3 Commando,
he had been one of the first chosen to take
part in the regiment's re-formation during the
Emergency in Malaya. From there he had returned
to Bradbury Lines, then still located at Merebrook
Camp, Malvern, where he had worked with his
former Malayan Squadron Commander, Major
Pryce-Jones, on the structuring of the rigorous
new Selection and Training programme for the
regiment, based mostly on ideas devised and thor-
oughly tested in Malaya. Promoted to the rank of
Major in 1962, shortly after the SAS had transferred to Bradbury Lines, Hereford, Callaghan had
been pleased to be offered the leadership of D
Squadron just before its assignment to the Borneo
campaign in 1964.

It is possible, therefore, that he felt even more at
peace with the world because some of his former
troopers, including the so-called 'troublemakers'

Pete Welsh and Alf Laughton, both since promoted to corporal, and Corporal (now Sergeant) Richard Parker, were here with him, impatiently waiting for the briefing while wiping sweat from their faces and swatting away swarms of flies and mosquitoes.

'Piggin' fucking flies and mosquitoes,' Alf Laughton said. 'They only send me to countries filled with the bastards. It's their way of tormenting me and driving me loopy.'

'You buzz like a fly and whine like a mosquito,' his good mate, Pete Welsh, replied sardonically. 'That's why they send you to places like this. They think they're sending you home.'

'Fuck you an' all,' Alf grunted.

'All right,' Callaghan said firmly, picking up a pointer, tapping it noisily on his lectern, then pulling the cloth covering off the blackboard behind him to reveal a large map of Borneo. 'Pay attention now. This,' he continued when the men had settled down, 'is what we're protecting.' He tapped the word 'Sarawak' with his pointer, then 'Kuching' and 'Brunei' and finally ran the pointer along the red-dotted line marking the border. 'Regarding the required background . . .'

He was interrupted by the customary moans and groans, since this was always the least popular part of an initial briefing, when the men had to listen, rather than taking part in the SAS custom of the

'Chinese parliament', or free exchange of ideas between officers and men.

'I know you all find this boring,' Callaghan said, grinning, 'but it's necessary, so kindly be quiet.' When they had settled down again, he continued: 'Brunei is one of three British dependencies in Borneo; the others are the colonies of North Borneo, now known as Sabah, and Sarawak. These territories, though extensive, represent only a quarter of the island. The rest belongs to Indonesia, whose head of state, President Sukarno . . .'

'The Mad Doctor!' Alf bellowed, winning a few laughs. With flaming red hair and a face pitted by acne, the corporal looked like a wild man. He had served twice in Malaya. The first time was in 1953 with the King's Own Yorkshire Light Infantry – when he had spent most of his time having a good time in Penang, rather than fighting. The second was in 1958, when, as a recently badged SAS trooper, he had been forced to stop fooling around and, instead, faced the horrors of the Telok Anson swamp alongside Sergeant Parker, Corporal Pete Welsh and a good many other, now dead, friends. Once considered a troublemaker and almost thrown out of the SAS, Alf had been saved by his exemplary behaviour in that dreadful swamp and went on to become a ruthlessly efficient member of the Directing Staff at 22 SAS Training

Wing, Hereford. Now considered an 'old Malayan hand', he was indisputably a good man to have in Borneo.

'Yes,' Callaghan agreed, acknowledging the nickname bestowed by British troops on Indonesia's ambitious leader. 'The Mad Doctor . . . Anyway, on 8 December 1962 an internal rebellion in Brunei was organized and led by a young sheikh named Azahart, who wanted to unite the three dependencies. This he did by launching simultaneous guerrilla attacks against police stations, government buildings and other strategically important targets. Obliged to put this revolt down, the British quickly sent in troops stationed in Singapore, including the Queen's Own Highlanders, the Royal Marine Commandos and the Gurkhas. Eight days later the rebellion was over and most of the rebels had fled into the jungle.'

'Where they remain to this day,' Pete Welsh said.

'More or less,' answered Callaghan.

Another old Malayan hand, Londoner Pete Welsh was an explosives expert who had been trained at No 101 Special Training School Singapore during World War Two, transferred as a sapper to 3rd Corps, with whom he had fought the Japanese during the occupation, then finally became an SAS trooper with D Squadron, returning to Malaya to take part in the Emergency with Alf Laughton, as well as some other good friends, who were killed in the Telok Anson swamp. Like Alf, regarded at that time as troublesome, he had, just like his mate, been matured by his experiences in the swamp and emerged to become an exemplary member of the Directing Staff at 22 SAS Training Wing. He was glad to be in Borneo, back in the thick of things.

'Which brings us to the Mad Doctor,' Alf said.

'Correct,' Callaghan replied. 'President Sukarno, a great fan of the Japanese, is now driven by the dream of unifying south-east Asia under a single leadership – naturally, in this case, his own – and has cast his greedy gaze on Borneo. For this reason, when Britain backed the proposed formation of a new political entity in the region, comprising Malaya, Singapore, Sabah, Sarawak and Brunei, Sukarno opposed it, did everything in his power to wreck the plan and, in December 1962, just after the Brunei Revolt had been put down, infiltrated insurgents from Kalimantan into Borneo. When, in September 1963, Sabah and Sarawak were officially incorporated into the new Malaysian Federation, Sukarno's forces dramatically increased their activities, with more attacks along the border. The British response was, again, immediate: to fly a force of Malaysian, British and Commonwealth troops in to contain the insurgents. You men are a further part of that force.'

The last comment was followed by a round of applause, handshaking, mutual backslapping and mutual congratulation. Callaghan let the hubbub die down before continuing: 'The jungle war, or so-called "Confrontation", between Britain and Indonesia is being fought on our part with a mixed force of Gurkhas, Australians and New Zealanders, totalling about 28,000 men. It's being fought in an area as intractable as Vietnam or – for those old hands present – Malaya.'

'If we did it in Malaya,' Pete Welsh said, 'we can do it here.'

'Hear, hear!' a few of the men chimed.

Callaghan grinned and nodded, acknowledging what they were saying, before adding a more cautious note. 'Let's hope so. However, please bear in mind that just as the CTs [communist terrorists] in Malaya were wizards in the jungle, so President Sukarno's Indonesian troops are sea-soned experts in this largely unexplored jungle region.'

'Not as expert as us,' Pete said stubbornly. 'We can match anyone in the *ulu*.'

'Right,' Alf agreed.

Callaghan grinned, then continued: 'The original purpose of Sukarno's troops was to destabilize the fledgling Federation of Malaysia through clandestine guerrilla warfare and terrorism. However, when that failed, Sukarno's generals turned to all-out invasion and blatant warfare, including air attacks on the Malay Peninsula and incursions along the border between Indonesian-held Kalimantan and Sarawak. Our job is to stop that.'

'How?' Sergeant Richard Parker asked in his chillingly quiet manner. Glancing down from the dais, Callaghan saw the grey eyes of Parker gazing up at him, unblinking and, to some, unnerving.

Parker was universally known as 'Dead-eye Dick' or simply 'Dead-eye' because of his exceptional marksmanship – displayed not only during his three years with the 2nd Battalion, Royal Regiment of Fusiliers, but also on the firing range of the SAS base at Merebrook Camp, Malvern, and then, most notably, during the Malayan Emergency of 1958. As Callaghan knew only too well, Dead-eye had gone into that campaign a rather quiet, serious young man who desperately wanted to be a good SAS trooper and had emerged, after some dreadful experiences in the Telok Anson swamp, an even quieter, emotionally withdrawn man but a superlative soldier.

Promoted to corporal as a reward for the bravery and skill he had displayed in Malaya, particularly in the swamp, Dead-eye had moved with the Regiment from Malvern to Hereford, where he acted as a somewhat restless member of the Directing Staff, clearly yearning for another war to fight. Bored with the peace-time fighting force, he had married a girl he met in Hereford, but separated from her three years later. By 1963, when he had been posted with the squadron to Borneo, the marriage was over.

Callaghan thought he knew why. For a long time after returning from Malaya, Dead-eye had been haunted by his appalling experiences in the Telok Anson swamp, in particular the death of the man he had most respected and tried to emulate, Sergeant Lorrimer, whose head had been guillotined by a female CT wielding a *parang*, a machete-like jungle knife. This gruesome scene had taken place right in front of Dead-eye.

Subsequently, back in Malvern, then in Hereford, Dead-eye had suffered repeated nightmares about the severed head of Lorrimer, whose eyes (so Dead-eye reported to the SAS psychiatrist) had kept moving frantically left and right in his head for some time after it had been severed. This bizarre phenomenon had been caused by a final, perfectly natural, nervous spasm of the muscles controlling the eyeballs, but to Dead-eye it had seemed that Lorrimer was still alive in some way and desperate to know what had happened to him – or, worse still, pleading for release from his nightmare.

More than anything else, it was the recollection of that severed head and its desperately swivelling eyes that had haunted Dead-eye for years afterwards and probably made him impossible to live with. It could not have helped the marriage; in fact, it had almost certainly ended it.

'The main problem facing Major-General W. Walker, the British commander in Borneo,' Callaghan replied, speaking directly to Dead-eye, 'is that he has only five battalions to cover more than 1000 miles of jungle-covered border. Also, in addition to Sukarno's Indonesian insurgents, he has to contend with an internal threat in the shape of the Clandestine Communist Organization, composed mainly of Chinese settlers from Sarawak. Initially, General Walker wanted us to act as a kind of mobile reserve, dropping onto the jungle canopy by parachute, as we did in Malaya, but this was deemed too dangerous and unlikely to produce worthwhile results. Instead, we'll be operating in small patrols along the border, not engaging with the enemy unless absolutely necessary, but providing early warning of any Indonesian or CCO incursions.'

As most of the men hated R & I, as distinct from direct engagement, this announcement received the expected moans and groans, eventually silenced by a question from Pete Welsh.

'We've virtually just arrived here,' he said, 'so know little about what's going on. Who else is involved in this conflict? Sorry, boss, *confrontation!*'

Callaghan grinned at Pete's mockery of the official term, then became serious again. 'As Malaysia is a member of the South-East Asia Treaty Organization, the Aussie and Kiwi SAS have each sent us a squadron. The Kiwis, in particular – perhaps because of the large number of Maoris in their ranks – are the best jungle trackers we've got. I would ask you men of D Squadron – fresh as you are from training in West Germany and Norway and, in many cases, experienced as you are from your excellent work during the Emergency in Malaya – to be on your best behaviour with them.'

This was greeted with hoots of derisive laughter, which Callaghan deliberately ignored.

'Also, having arrived here a few months before us, A Squadron has renewed old friendships with veterans of the Sarawak Rangers, Iban tribal trackers and headhunters brought to the Malay Peninsula in the 1950s as teachers and pupils of the SAS during the campaign.'

One of the new men, Private Terry Malkin,

nervously put his hand up, cleared his throat and said, "Scuse me, boss!'

'Yes?'

'What did you mean when you said that the natives were teachers *and* pupils?'

Malkin, only recently badged and still nervous with the old hands, was a Signaller. As he came from Northern Ireland, the other troopers often joked that he should be particularly good as a radio operator, blessed as he surely was with Celtic intuition and 'second sight'. A lot of jokes bounced off Malkin's hide on those spurious grounds.

'We taught them about modern firearms and soldiering; they taught us about tracking in the jungle. Since coming here, A Squadron has been using them as a paramilitary force, the Sarawak Rangers, later known as the Border Scouts, but that's being changed. From now on they'll be used solely as trackers and support units to SAS-led Gurkha teams.'

'Why?' Dead-eye asked.

'Last September our Scout post at Long Jawi, located near the border of Sarawak, was attacked and destroyed by over a hundred Indonesian soldiers who'd crossed the border from Kalimantan. Most of those men approached the post by boat, but according to the sole survivor of the attack, Corporal Ralph Sanderson, some of them emerged from the kampong itself, which they must have infiltrated days before.'

At the mention of Sanderson's name, practically everyone in the room glanced automatically at the lean-faced soldier sitting in the back row, ignoring the flies and mosquitoes swarming around him. He was obviously used to them.

'Though he came to Borneo with A Squadron,' Callaghan explained, 'Corporal Sanderson has been transferred to D Squadron to give us the benefit of his experience. If any of you men have any questions to put to him at any time over the next few months, don't hesitate. For the moment, however, please limit yourselves to any questions you might have for me regarding the briefing so far.'

'How did we react to the attack against Long Jawi?' Dead-eye asked.

'Swiftly and effectively,' Callaghan replied without hesitation. 'We flew Gurkhas to cut-off points on the Indonesians' line of retreat, where most of the enemy were killed in ambushes. Nevertheless, the fact that the Dyaks had not mentioned their presence, and that the Border Scouts failed to lend adequate support to the few Gurkhas in the post, made it perfectly clear that we can't depend on the former for anything other than tracking and intelligence gathering. Their training has therefore been taken over by the Gurkha Independent Parachute Company. Also, they no longer wear uniforms, which makes them less obviously members of the Security Forces. Naturally, we'll still use them as porters or to fell trees to clear helicopter LZs, as they're expert at both those tasks.'

'What about us?' Alf asked.

'Since the Indonesian forces are making more frequent incursions into Sarawak and Sabah, we'll be living almost entirely in the jungle, this time relying on our Border Scouts only for local information or when visiting a longhouse for a brief stay. Once we've settled in among the indigenous population, our function will be to patrol the areas where the Indonesians are most likely to cross the border. These include the comparatively flat plains along Sarawak's western border; the valley tracks leading through Stass, about 30 miles from Kuching, the capital of Sarawak; the previously mentioned Long Jawi in the 3rd Division; the valleys south of Pensiamgan; and the waterways of eastern Sabah.'

Dead-eye turned his flat, grey gaze on Corporal Sanderson. 'Speaking from experience, what's your judgement on the Indo incursions?'

Sanderson smiled slightly, recognizing a kindred soul. 'It's my belief,' he replied with confidence, 'that small Indonesian patrols also infiltrate by other, less visible routes, particularly in the unexplored stretch of jungle known as 'the Gap', lying east of the Pensiamgan valleys of Sabah.'

'Precisely,' Callaghan interjected. 'The Gap! Though largely unexplored territory, therefore particularly dangerous, that area will become your main battle zone.'

'I thought we weren't engaging the enemy,' Alf said sarcastically.

'You know what I mean, Trooper. If engagement is unavoidable, you engage; otherwise these are R & I patrols.'

'How do we insert?' Terry Malkin asked.

'A good question from our most recently badged member!' Callaghan responded, only half joking and going on to give a serious explanation. 'We insert in small groups by chopper to an LZ within yomping distance of the respective target kampongs. From there we march the rest of the way. Once at their selected kampong, the individual small groups will ingratiate themselves slowly but surely, adopting a hearts-and-minds approach, as we did in Malaya. Finally, when the trust of the aboriginals has been gained, you will persuade them to let us bring more troops in by helicopter – the regular Army, Royal Marine Commandos and Gurkhas – to turn the kampongs into fortified camps. Once that's done, we start sending

SAS-led R & I patrols out into the surrounding jungle – either with or without the help of the natives.'

'What are the hazards of this particular jungle?' Terry asked, obviously taking this, his first campaign, very seriously.

Callaghan simply glanced at Sanderson, who said without a trace of irony: 'Snakes, lizards, leeches, wild pigs, aggressive boar and primitive peoples: Land and Sea Dyaks, Muruts and Punans. Some of them are headhunters and don't take too kindly to strangers.'

'And we're using them as trackers?' the trooper asked doubtfully.

Sanderson grinned. 'Only the ones we know and have personally trained. Others, when not actually headhunting, work for the Indos or CCO, so you have to be careful.'

'*When* do we insert?' Dead-eye asked.

'The day after tomorrow,' Major Callaghan replied. 'Today you rest; tomorrow you prepare; the next day you leave. The flight is only twenty minutes. When you reach your LZ, an NCO from A Squadron will be there to take you in to the selected kampong and guide you through the hearts-and-minds requirements for this particular area. Any more questions?'

'Yes,' Pete Welsh said. 'I'm told that the natives

often offer their bare-breasted daughters as gifts. Are we allowed to accept?'

'The elders are genuine when they offer,' Sanderson replied from the last row, 'but if you accept the offer, you're liable to offend the young men of the kampong. The short answer, then, is a categorical no!'

A loud chorus of exaggerated groans filled the room, followed by Alf's melodramatic: 'War is hell!'

'You should know,' Callaghan responded. 'That's it. Class dismissed!'

The men gratefully pushed back their chairs and hurried out of the briefing room, determined to enjoy their last day of rest before the hard work began.

2

Selected as one team were Sergeant Parker, Corporals Welsh and Laughton, Private Malkin, all of D Squadron, and A Squadron's Corporal Sanderson, who would be their general guide and adviser, both in the jungle and regarding their relationship with the Dyaks.

After their day of rest, which took the form of a lengthy booze-up in the NAAFI, they arose at first light to shower, shave, dress, have a hearty breakfast, then get kitted out with proper jungle wear. This included 'olive-greens'; a soft, peaked hat with sweat-band and a yellow marker inside for identification; and rubber-and-canvas jungle boots with a metal plate inserted in the sole to prevent sharp objects, such as vicious *punji* stakes, going through the sole and into the foot. The kit consisted of ammunition pouches; two external water bottles; and the usual bergen rucksack including, in this instance, a useful bamboo carrier, two spare water bottles, a rolled-up sleeping bag, canvas sheeting and camouflaged hessian for setting up a temporary 'basha', and an escape belt holding high-calorie rations, hexamine fuel blocks, a fishing line and hooks, a small knife, waterproofed matches, a button-compass and a small-scale map.

Private Malkin was given a standard-issue Armalite M16 5.56mm assault rifle with 20-round box magazine, Corporal Sanderson opted for the generally less popular 7.62mm SLR, which he insisted he was used to, and the rest selected the 7.62mm Armalite assault rifle, which was light and compact, and therefore ideally suited to the jungle. Each man was also given a good supply of '36' hand-grenades and '80' white-phosphorus incendiary grenades, which were clipped to the webbed belts around their chests and waist. All of them were also given a standard-issue 9mm Browning High Power handgun with 13-round magazines and a Len Dixon holster. They were also given two knives, a Fairburn-Sykes commando knife and a *parang*.

'Shit,' Terry said, swinging the Malay jungle knife experimentally from left to right, 'this thing looks pretty dangerous.'

'We first had these in Malaya,' Alf told him, 'and a lot of us badly cut ourselves while learning to use them. It isn't as easy as it looks, so handle that item with care, kid.'

'Yes, boss.' Terry clipped the sheathed *parang* to his belt, beside the commando knife. 'I feel as heavy as an elephant with all this gear.'

'You'll soon get used to it, Trooper.'

Though every member of the four-man patrol had been trained in signals, demolition and medicine, and was presently undergoing training in the local language, each individual had to specialize in one of these skills. Trained to Regimental Signaller standard in Morse code and ciphers, the team's specialist signaller was responsible for calling in aerial resup (resupply) missions, casualty evacuations and keeping contact with base. While all had been trained in demolition work, the team's specialist in this field was responsible for either supervising, or carrying out, major sabotage operations. The job of the language specialist was to converse with the locals, to both gain their trust as part of the hearts-and-minds campaign and gather any information he could glean from them. Last but not least, the specialist in medicine would not only look after the other members of his patrol but also attempt to win the trust of the locals by treating them for any illnesses, real or imagined, that they might complain of.

As the team's demolition expert, Pete Welsh was placed in charge of their single crate of mixed explosives, mostly of the plastic type such as RDX and PETN, along with both kinds of initiator: electrical and non-electrical, with the relevant firing caps and time fuses. As signaller, Terry was not asked to depend on his Celtic clairvoyance but instead was given an A41 British Army tactical radio set, which weighed 11lb excluding the battery and was carried in a backpack. Each of the men was supplied with a SARBE (surface-to-air rescue beacon) lightweight radio beacon to enable them to link up with CasEvac helicopters should the need arise.

Having been trained in first-aid and basic medicine, each man in the patrol was obliged to carry an individual medical pack that included codeine tablets and syrettes of morphine; mild and strong antiseptics (gentian violet and neomycin sulphate); chalk and opium for diarrhoea and other intestinal disorders; the antibiotic tetracycline; and an assortment of dressings and plasters. However, as the team's medical specialist, more extensively trained with the US Army's special forces at Fort Sam, Houston, Texas, and Fort Bragg, North Carolina, Alf was in charge of a comprehensive medical pack that included all the above items, but also a greater selection of drugs and dressings, as well as surgical equipment and a dental repair kit.

'I wouldn't let that butcher near *my* mouth, Pete

33

said, 'if my teeth were hanging out by the roots. I'd rather pull 'em myself.'

'Any more sarcastic remarks,' Alf retorted, 'and I'll practise my surgery on your balls instead of your teeth. I'm pretty good when it comes to the cut and thrust, so don't cross me, mate.'

'Another mad doctor,' Pete replied. 'We should call you Sukarno.'

As the team's linguist, Dead-eye carried the lightest load. But once in the jungle, which was usually known by the native word *ulu*, he would compensate for this by being out front on 'point', as scout – the most dangerous and demanding job of them all.

Sanderson, as their guest, or rather guide, carried only his personal weapons and kit.

Kitted out just after breakfast, the men were then compelled to spend the rest of the long, hot morning on the firing range, testing the weapons and honing their skills. This was not as easy as it sounds, for the heat soon became suffocating, sweat ran constantly down their foreheads and into their eyes when they took aim, and they often choked on the dust kicked up by the backblast of the weapons. On top of all this, they were tormented by the usual swarms of flies and mosquitoes.

'I give up,' Alf said. 'I can't even see along

the sights with these clouds of bloody insects everywhere. Let's just call it a day.'

'Get back on your belly on the ground,' Dead-eye said. 'And don't get up till I say so.'

'Yes, Sarge!' Alf snapped.

They came off the firing range covered in a fine slime composed of their own sweat and the dust. After a refreshing shower, they washed the clothes they had used on the firing range, hung them up to drip dry in the still-rising heat, dressed in their spare set of olive-greens, then hurried to the mess for lunch. This was followed by an afternoon of lessons about the history, geography and culture of Borneo, with particular emphasis on the border between Sarawak and Kalimantan, where most of their operations would take place.

By the time the lessons had ended, in the late afternoon, the men's clothes had dried and could be ironed (which they did themselves), then packed away in the bergens. When their packing was completed, they had dinner in the mess, followed by precisely one hour in the bar, which ensured that they could not drink too much.

Back in the spider, or sleeping quarters, each man had to take his place beside his bed, while Dead-eye inspected his kit and weapons, ensuring that no bergen was too heavy and that the weapons were immaculately clean and in perfect working order.

Satisfied, he told them to be up and ready to leave by first light the following morning, then bid them goodnight and left the barracks.

When Dead-eye had gone Terry exhaled with an audible sigh. 'Blimey!' he almost gasped. 'That Sergeant Parker scares the hell out of me. He's so bloody expressionless.'

'A born killer,' Alf said gravely.

'Heart of stone,' Pete added.

'He eats new boys like you for breakfast,' Alf warned. 'I'd be careful if I was you.'

'Aw, come on, lads!' Terry protested, not sure if they were serious or not. 'I mean . . .'

'Never look him directly in the eye,' Pete said firmly.

'Never speak to him unless spoken to,' Alf chipped in.

'If you see him take a deep breath,' Pete continued, 'hold onto your balls.'

'He'll bite them off otherwise,' Alf said, 'then spit them out in your face.'

'Leave off, you two!'

'It's the truth,' Pete said.

'Cross our hearts,' Alf added. 'Old Parker, he'd cut your throat as soon as look at you, so it's best to avoid him.'

'How can I avoid him?' Terry asked. 'He's our *patrol leader*, for God's sake! I mean, he's going to be there every minute, breathing right in my face.'

'And he *does* so hate new troopers,' Pete said. 'You can take that as read.'

'You poor bastard,' Alf said.

Terry was starting to look seriously worried when Alf, able to control himself no longer, rolled over on his bed to smother his laughter in his pillow.

'Night-night,' Pete said chirpily, then he switched out the lights.

At dawn the next morning, after a hurried breakfast, they were driven in a Bedford RL 4x4 three-ton lorry to the airfield, where they transferred to a stripped-out Wessex Mark 1 helicopter piloted by Lieutenant Ralph Ellis of the Army Air Corps. Some of them knew Ellis from Malaya five years before, when he had flown them into the Telok Anson swamp in his Sikorsky S-55 Whirlwind.

'You men haven't aged a day,' Ellis greeted them. 'You *always* looked like a bunch of geriatrics.'

'Listen who's talking,' Pete countered. 'Nice little bald spot you've developed in five years. Soon you'll be nothing but ears and head while we remain beautiful.'

'The girls still love the pilots,' Ellis replied. 'They

37

don't view us as hooligans in uniform. They think we have class.'

'And what's this?' Alf asked, poking Ellis in the stomach with his forefinger. 'A nice bit of flab here.'

'It's the easy life the bastard lives,' Pete informed his mate. 'He'll soon look like a cute little blanc-mange with a billiard ball on top.'

'Very funny, I'm sure,' Ellis replied. 'Just get your fat arses in the chopper, thanks.'

'Yes, mother!' Alf and Pete replied as one, grinning wickedly as they clambered into the Wessex, followed by the others. Once inside, the men strapped themselves in, cramped together among the mass of equipment. The engines roared into life and the props started spinning. The heli-copter shuddered as if about to fall apart, rose vertically until it was well above the treetops, then headed west, flying over a breathtaking panorama of densely forested hills and mountain peaks, winding rivers, waterfalls, swamps, aerial bridges and shadowy, winding paths through the *ulu*.

'That jungle looks impenetrable from here,' Terry observed, glancing down through the win-dow in disbelief.

'In many places it is,' Alf replied, 'but we'll manage somehow.'

Twenty minutes later the Wessex landed in

a jungle clearing and the men disembarked, to be greeted by another member of A Squadron, Sergeant Alan Hunt. Dropped on his own a week ago, he was living in the clearing, close to a stone-filled, gurgling river, his basha a poncho pegged diagonally from the lowest branch of a tree to the ground with his kit piled neatly up inside. Hunt was wearing jungle-green trousers and a loose shirt that seemed far too big for him. A Browning High Power handgun was holstered on his hip.

'Hi, boss,' Sanderson said, shaking the sergeant's hand. 'Boy, have *you* lost a lot of weight already!'

The sergeant grinned and shrugged. 'Three stone fell off me just living here for two weeks. You'll all look the same soon enough.' He indicated the clearing with a wave of his right hand and all of them, glancing around at the oblique beams of sunlight streaking the gloom, realized just how hot and humid it was. 'Ditch your gear and fix up your bashas. This is home for the next week or so. I'm sure you'll enjoy it. When you're ready, gather around my lean-to and I'll tell you what's happening.'

When the helicopter had taken off again and its slipstream had died down, the men followed Hunt's example by constructing triangular shelters with their waterproof ponchos, first hammering two

Y-shaped sticks into the ground about six feet apart, running a length of rope between them and tying the rope tight, then draping the poncho over the rope and pegging the ends down to form a triangular tent. A groundsheet was rolled out inside the tent and covered with dry grass to make a mattress. A sleeping bag was then rolled out on the grass to make a soft bed. All of the lean-tos were well hidden by clumps of bamboo and screened from above by the soaring trees.

When their kit had been placed carefully around the inner edges of the tent, the men lit their hexamine stoves outside and brewed up. They drank their tea gathered around Hunt, hearing what he had been up to since arriving there a fortnight earlier.

'As most of you know,' he began, 'when waging our hearts-and-minds campaign in Malaya, we transplanted the aboriginals from their original kampongs into new, fortified villages, well out of reach of the CTs. Given the nature of the locals, as well as the terrain, there's no possibility of doing that here. In any case, most of the tribesmen are well disposed towards the British and we have to capitalize on that by relying on non-violent persuasion and using them where they live, rather than attempting to move them on. To this end I've already made contact with the elders of the nearby kampong, which is about five minutes from here.'

He pointed at the dense jungle to his left.

'My first step towards penetration was to build this hide within walking distance of the kampong. From here, I kept the village under observation long enough to ensure that neither guerrillas nor Indonesian regulars were already established there. Once I was sure that they weren't, I walked in, all smiles, and made contact through a combination of basic Malay and sign language. Gradually, they came to accept me and I started helping them with modest medical aid and by bartering some of my possessions for some of theirs. Now that I've been accepted, I can introduce you as friends and hopefully you'll win their trust the same way, gradually becoming part of the village and sharing their lifestyle. Once that's been accomplished, we'll persuade them that our other friends should be invited in, too. If they agree, we can then call in the regular Army and Gurkhas – all one big happy family. We then use the village as a Forward Operating Base, moving out on regular patrols into the *ulu*, hopefully with the help of the villagers.'

'What are they like as people?' Dead-eye asked.

'Physically small, generally cheerful, and lazy.'

'Sounds just like me!' Pete quipped.

'They don't cut their hair,' Hunt continued,

ignoring the quip. 'Nor do they dress above the waist – neither the men nor the women – so you'll have to learn not to let the females distract you too much.'

'I'm willing to die for my country,' Alf said, 'but what you're asking is too much.'

'I'm very serious about this,' Hunt said sharply. 'Certain proprieties have to be maintained here, no matter how you might feel to the contrary. For instance, the village elders have a tendency to offer their daughters as a gesture of goodwill. You won't get into trouble if you politely refuse. However, you *may* get into trouble if you accept.'

'My heart's breaking already,' Pete said. 'I know just what's coming.'

'Although, as I've said, the natives are generally cheerful, the young men suffer jealousy like the rest of us mere mortals and could take offence if you take their girls. In short, if you receive such an offer, make sure you refuse.'

'What kind of gifts should we give them?' Terry asked, as solemn as ever.

'You don't. Generally speaking, the Malay system of giving gifts doesn't work here, though bartering of a minor nature is enjoyed. Instead, what you do is be mindful of their pride, showing tact, courtesy, understanding and, most of all, patience regarding all aspects of their lifestyle.

Also, it's vitally important that you show respect for the headman, whose dignity and prestige have to be upheld at all times. Obey those few simple rules and you should have no problems.'

'So when do we start?' Dead-eye asked.

'Today,' Hunt replied. 'At least one man has to stay here to guard the camp at all times – this will be a rotating duty – while the others go into the kampong. As Corporal Sanderson is already familiar with the Indians, he'll stay here today and the rest of you can come in with me. Leave your weapons here in Sanderson's care, then let's get up and go.'

'We're going straight away?' Terry asked, looking uneasy.

'That's right, Trooper. What's your problem?'

'He's embarrassed at the thought of seeing all those bare boobs,' Pete said, making Terry blush a deep crimson.

'Cherry-boy, is he?' Hunt asked crisply.

'No!' Terry replied too quickly. 'I'm not. I just . . .'

'Think you'll get a hard-on as soon as you see those bare tits,' Pete interjected, giving form to Terry's thoughts. 'Well, no harm in that, son!'

'Just keep your thoughts above the waist – yours, that is,' the sergeant said, 'and you should be all right. OK, men, let's go.'

43

As Sanderson stretched out on the grassy ground beside his basha and lit up a cigarette, the others extinguished the flames from the burning hexamine blocks in their portable cookers, then followed Hunt into the dense undergrowth. Surprisingly, they found themselves walking along a narrow, twisting path, barely distinguishable in the gloom beneath the overhanging foliage.

Terry, the least experienced in the group, immediately felt oppressed and disorientated by the *ulu*. He had stepped into a vast silence that made his own breathing – even his heartbeat – seem unnaturally loud. Instead of the riot of birds, wildlife, flowers and natural colours he had expected, he found only a sunless gloom deepened by the dark green and brown of vine stems, tree-ferns, snake-like coils of rattan, an abundance of large and small palms, long, narrow, dangerously spiked leaves, gnarled, knotted branches – and everywhere brown mud. Glancing up from the featureless jungle, he was oppressed even more by the sheer size of the trees which soared above the dense foliage to dizzying heights, forming vertical tunnels of green and brown, the great trunks entangled in yet more liana and vine, disappearing into the darkness of their own canopy, blotting out the sunlight.

Looking up, Terry felt even more dizzy and disorientated. In that great silent and featureless

44

gloom, he felt divorced from his own flesh and blood. His racing heart shocked him.

Though the hike took only five minutes, it seemed much longer than that, and Terry sighed with relief when the group emerged into the relative brightness of an unreal grey light that fell down through a window in the canopy of the trees on the thatched longhouses of the kampong spread out around the muddy banks of the river. The dwellings were raised on stilts, piled up one behind the other, each slightly above the other, on the wooded slopes climbing up from the river. Some, Terry noticed with a tremor, had shrunken human heads strung above their doors. The spaces below and between the houses, where the ground had been cleared for cultivation, were filled with the Iban villagers – also known as Sea Dyaks because they had once been pirates – who, stripped to the waist, male and female, young and old, were engaged in a variety of tasks, such as cooking, fishing, laundering, picking jungle fruit – figs, durians, bananas and mangos – or working in a small, dry *padi*, where their basic food, rice and tapioca, was grown. This they did with no great expenditure of energy, except when playing odd games and giggling. Their longboats were tied up to a long, rickety jetty, bobbing and creaking noisily in the water. Buffalo and pigs also congregated there, drinking the water or eating the tall grass as chickens squawked noisily about them.

'They fish in that river,' Hunt explained. 'They also hunt wild pig, deer, birds, monkeys and other animals, using traps and the odd shotgun, but mostly blowpipes that fire poisoned arrows. Annoy them and they'll fire them at you – so don't steal their women!'

Terry was blushing deeply, Pete and Alf were gawping, and Dead-eye was staring impassively as a group of bare-breasted women, giggling and nudging each other, approached behind a very old, wizened man who was naked except for a loincloth and, incongruously, a pair of British army jungle boots. Obviously the headman, he raised a withered arm, spread the fingers of his hand, and croaked the one word of English he had learned from Sergeant Hunt: 'Welcome!'

Two weeks later, Terry had stopped blushing at the sight of the bare-breasted women, but felt even more disorientated and removed from himself. This had begun with his first short trek through the awesome silence and gloom of the *ulu*, but was deepened by his daily visits to the kampong and his increasingly intimate interaction with the Ibans. They were so gentle and good-natured that he could not imagine them as pirates, let alone as the headhunters they obviously were, judging by the shrunken heads on prominent display. Certainly, however, they lived a primitive life of fishing in the rivers, hunting animals with blowpipes, tilling the kampong's one rice-and-tapioca *padi*, and constantly maintaining their longhouses with raw materials from the jungle. They also engaged in amiable barter, trading jungle products such as timber, rattan, rice, tapioca, fruit, fish, even the swiftlet's nests used for Chinese soup, in return for clothes, boots, rifles, tins of baked beans, chewing gum and cigarettes. Bartering, from the point of view of the SAS troopers, was the easiest way to the affections of the villagers, leading to much giggling and backslapping.

Once this had become commonplace, however, the men started winning the hearts and minds of the Ibans in other ways: Pete showed them how to use explosives for various small tasks, such as blowing fish out of the water; Alf ran a daily open-air clinic to deal with their real and imagined illnesses; Terry entertained them by tuning his short-wave radio into various stations, which invariably reduced them to excited giggles; Dead-eye trained some of them in the selective use of weapons; and Hunt and Sanderson took turns with Dead-eye to teach English to the more important men of the kampong.

47

The SAS men spent most of their waking hours with the Ibans, which made for a long and exhausting day. Invariably, this began at first light when, just after breakfast, they would make the short hike through the *ulu* from their hidden camp to the kampong. After an average of twelve hours in the kampong, eating their lunch with the Ibans, they would make their way back to the camp, invariably at last light and concealing their tracks as they went, to have a brew-up and feed gratefully off compo rations.

The Ibans were very sociable, and often, in the interests of good manners and improved relations, the troopers would be obliged to stay in one of the longhouses to partake of native hospitality. For all of them, this was pure torture, particularly since the villagers' favourite meal was a stinking mess called *jarit*, which they made by splitting a length of thick bamboo, filling it with raw pork, salt and rice, and burying it for a month until it had putrefied. Indeed, while Dead-eye and Hunt were able to digest this stinking mess without bother, the others could only do so without throwing up by washing it down with mouthfuls of *tapai*, a fierce rice wine which looked like unfermented cider, scalded the throat and led to monumental hangovers. Nevertheless, when drunk through straws from large Chinese jars, it was potent

48

enough to drown the stench and foul taste of the *jarit*.

The eating and drinking, combined with the accompanying entertainments, in which the SAS men were obliged to dance for the villagers, was made no easier by the fact that many families shared a single longhouse and the air was fetid not only from their sweat and the heat. Also, because they used the floor as a communal toilet, urinating and defecating through the slatted floor onto the ground below, the purgent air was thick at all times with swarms of flies and mosquitoes.

Luckily for the SAS men, they were called upon to explore the surrounding area and fill in the blank spaces on their maps, showing waterways suitable for boat navigation, tracks that could be classified as main or secondary, distances both in linear measurements and marching hours, contours and accessibility of specific areas, primary and secondary jungle (*belukar*), and swamps, and areas under cultivation (*ladang*). They also filled their logbooks with often seemingly irrelevant, though actually vitally important, details about the locals' habits and customs, their food, their state of health, the variety of their animals, their weapons and their individual measure of importance within the community. Last but not least, they marked down potential ambush positions, border crossing-points, and suitable locations for parachute droppings and helicopter landings. While this work was all conducted in the suffocating humidity of the *ulu*, it was preferable to socializing in the fetid longhouses.

By the end of the two weeks, close relationships had been formed between the villagers and the SAS men, with the former willing to listen to the latter and do favours for them.

'The time's come to bring in the regular troops and fortify the kampong,' Sergeant Hunt informed Dead-eye. 'Then we can go out on proper jungle patrols, using the village as our FOB.'

'Do you think the locals will wear it?'

'That depends entirely on how we put it to them,' Hunt said with a relaxed grin. 'I think I know how to do that. First we tell them that evil men from across the mountain are coming and that we're here to protect the village. Then we explain that although our group is only five in number, we have many friends who'll descend from the sky, bringing aid. It would be particularly helpful, we'll then explain, if the necessary space could be created for the flying soldiers to land safely. I think that might work.'

'Let's try it,' Dead-eye said.

That afternoon they approached the village elders, joining them in the headman's longhouse, where they were compelled to partake of the foul-smelling *jarit*, mercifully washing it down with the scalding, highly alcoholic rice wine. After four hours of small talk, by which time both troopers were feeling drunk, Hunt put his case to the headman and received a toothless, drunken smile and nod of agreement. The headman then also agreed to have a landing space cleared for the flying soldiers to land on. Indeed, he and the others expressed great excitement at the thought of witnessing this heavenly arrival.

Immediately on leaving the longhouse, Hunt, trying not to show his drunkenness, told Terry to call up A Squadron and ask them to implement the 'step-up' technique devised by their brilliant commander, Major Peter de la Billière. This entailed warning a full infantry company to be ready to move by helicopter to a remote forward location for a demonstration of quick deployment and firepower.

The following day, when Hunt and Dead-eye were sober, the tribesmen expertly felled a large number of trees with small, flexible axes, dragged them away with ropes, then flattened the cleared area, thus carving a helicopter landing zone out of the jungle. When they had completed this task and were waiting excitedly around the edge of the LZ for the arrival of the 'flying soldiers', Hunt ordered Terry to radio the message: 'Bring in the step-up party now.' About fifteen minutes later the helicopters appeared above the treetops, creating a tremendous din and a sea of swirling foliage, before descending vertically into the clearing and disgorging many small, sombre Gurkhas, all armed with sharpened *kukris*, or curved machetes, and modern weapons. The next wave of choppers brought in Royal Marine Commandos, the regular Army, and the remainder of D Squadron, SAS, all of whom were armed to the teeth.

The Ibans giggled, shrieked with excitement, and finally applauded with waves and the swinging of their blowpipes. They viewed the arrival of the Security Forces as pure entertainment.

3

With the arrival of the full Security Forces complement, the fortification of the kampong was soon accomplished and it became, in effect, a Forward Operating Base complete with landing pads for the resup Wessex Mark 1 helicopters; riverside sangars manned with Bren light machine-guns and Gurkhas armed with 7.62mm SLRs; and defensive pits, or 'hedgehogs', encircled by thatch-and-bamboo-covered 40-gallon drums, bristling with 4.2-inch mortars and 7.62mm general-purpose machine-guns, or GPMGs.

The bartering of portable radios, simple medical aid and other items beloved by the villagers rapidly ensured that the SF troops became a welcome body of men within the community – so much so that eventually the natives were making endless requests for helicopter trips to outlying kampongs and help with the transportation to market, also by chopper, of their rice and tapioca, timber and even pigs and chickens. In short, they came to rely more on the soldiers and airmen than on their own civilian administration.

'Like living in fucking Petticoat Lane,' Alf said. 'If you don't know how to barter you're doomed. A right bunch of Jew-boys, this lot are.'

'Jew-boys in loinclothes,' Pete added. 'With long hair and a lot of weird tattoos. They'd look pretty normal in the East End, peddling their wares.'

'Do you mind?' Terry said.

'What's that, Trooper?' Pete asked.

'I don't think you should use terms like 'Jew-boys'. I think it's offensive.'

'But you're Irish!' Alf exclaimed.

'Just born there,' Terry corrected him.

'If you were born there, that makes you fucking Irish, so don't come it with me, Pat.'

'Don't call me Pat.'

'His name's *Paddy*,' Pete exclaimed.

'He must be an Irish Jew,' Alf responded, 'to be so concerned about this lot.'

'I'm not Jewish,' Terry said. 'I'm not really Irish either. I just happened to be born there, that's all, but my family moved to Liverpool when I was three, so I don't know any more about Ireland than you two. I'm not Irish, really, and I'm certainly not a Jew. I just dislike anti-Semitism, that's all.'

'The cocky bastard's just picked up his winged

dagger and already he thinks he can give us lectures. Makes you wonder, doesn't it?' said Pete.

'I just meant . . .' began Terry.

'Don't worry, kid,' Alf said in his kindly manner, 'we're not remotely offended. We just think you're a dumb prat.'

'Hear, hear,' Pete agreed.

Despite the sentiments of Alf and Pete, the SAS troopers, being already experienced in hearts-and-minds work, were very skilled at it. Major Callaghan, who loved life in the jungle and had revelled in kampong life ever since his Malayan days, made his contribution by flying out, at his own expense, hampers of Christmas food from Fortnum and Mason's of London, to supply the natives. Not surprisingly, Pete's only comment was: 'They eat better than we do. Spoiled rotten those Indians are.'

'Fortnum and Mason's, no less!' Alf exclaimed, his normally pink cheeks more flushed than normal. 'And here we poor bastards sit, getting sick on raw pork and tapioca. Makes you want to puke, doesn't it?'

Sergeant Hunt, on the other hand, being of a practical bent, made his personal contribution to village life by constructing a water-powered generator to provide the only electric light in thousands of square miles. This thrilled the villagers.

Not to be outdone, Corporal Sanderson, whose four-day trek through the jungle after the attack on Long Jawi the previous year had already gained him a great deal of respect among his fellow SAS troopers, dismantled his bergen and converted its metal frame into a still for making alcohol.

'He may be from A Squadron,' Pete said, 'but he's all right with me. Any man who can make a still from a rucksack has to be A1.'

'I'll drink to that,' Alf replied, sampling the brew from Sanderson's still. 'But then I'll drink to anything!'

While most of the men clearly enjoyed making such contributions to village life, they never lost sight of precisely why they were making them: to win the hearts and minds of the Ibans, and persuade them to favour the SF forces over those of President Sukarno or the CCO. The message that accompanied their contributions was therefore always the same.

'The Indonesians and the CCO are on the other side of the mountains and one day they'll cross them to destroy you,' Dead-eye, the language specialist, would solemnly inform the locals in their own tongue. 'We are here to protect you.'

Once they had managed to convince the villagers of this, the SAS men were able to convince them also that they must help themselves by staying alert for anything unusual seen in the *ulu*.

'Particularly the marks of rubber-soled boots,' Hunt explained to them. 'The sign of the Indo invader. If you see those, please tell us.'

'Yes, yes,' the village elders promised, perhaps not quite understanding what they were being asked to do. 'We understand. Welcome!'

They did, however, know enough to understand that they were receiving the good things of life from people who feared the Indonesians and CCO. For that reason, when asked if they could select certain of their number to be 'link-men' with the soldiers, they were quick to comply. Callaghan then placed those selected as link-men in the charge of the Gurkhas, who trained them in the use of certain weapons, but mainly used their natural talents for tracking and intelligence-gathering in the jungle. Though called the Border Scouts, like those who had gone before them, they were not destined to be used as fighting soldiers, but as aids on the reconnaissance and intelligence-gathering missions. Given modern weapons to carry – mostly World War Two 0.3-inch M1 carbines – they were more than happy to take part.

'They love those fucking rifles,' Pete observed, 'but they forget to keep them out of your face when they're loading and cocking.'

'Too right,' his mate Alf agreed. 'If they actually get to shoot the bloody things, they'll be shooting themselves.'

'Or us,' Pete replied.

'In the meantime,' Terry said, 'I'm keeping out of their way.'

'Very wise,' Pete told him.

The bare-breasted Iban women brought daily presents of fruit and vegetables, the men arrived to gossip and swap news, the children looked on, hoping for sweets or chewing gum, and the leaders of the community came to ask for, and offer, advice. The SF men therefore slipped as easily into the primitive rhythms of the day and seasons as the people themselves. Soon the cycle of planting, seeding and harvesting became part of the soldier's life itself, and the native customs, rites and celebrations as familiar as Bank Holidays back home.

'I can't really complain about all these holidays,' Alf said, 'but three days of drinking that awful *tapai* shit doesn't quite compensate for the loss of a good pint of bitter.'

'Between the *tapai* and that *jarit*,' Pete said, 'I've more snot coming out of my arse than coming out of my nose. These bloody Ibans don't know shite from shinola, but what can you do? I mean, we have to be nice to them.'

'Yeah,' Alf grunted. 'Keep them smiling or lose your head. Those primitive bastards collect human heads like we collect postage stamps. So be nice to them. Yes, sir!'

'It's your job,' Terry said.

'What?' Alf asked, puzzled.

'It's part of the hearts-and-minds campaign,' Terry explained with studied patience, 'so it's part of your job. Apart from that, they good people and don't need your insults.'

'Insults?' Pete was outraged. 'Who the fuck's insulting them? We're just saying that they're primitive bastards and a pain in the arse.'

'That's the *jarit*,' Alf reminded him.

'Goes straight through you,' Pete said.

'Three days of eating *jarit* and drinking *tapai* and your guts are turned inside out.'

'Primitive bastards,' Pete repeated.

'Shit through the floorboards,' Alf reminded him.

'Of course, Paddy here – sorry, I mean Terry – thinks all that is wonderful.'

'The real world,' Alf said.

'Back to nature,' Pete explained.

'I'm just saying . . .' Terry began, then gave up. 'Oh, fuck off the pair of you!'

'We're corporals,' Alf said.

'And you're just a trooper,' Pete informed him.

SOLDIER H: SAS

'That means you're being insubordinate,' Alf
explained, 'and could go up on a charge.'

'Up you an' all,' Terry said.

While the SAS were attempting to win hearts
and minds, Gurkha teams of five or six men were
training ten or twenty times their own number
of tribesmen in counter-terrorist reconnaissance,
intelligence gathering and, less comprehensively,
warfare. The Gurkhas shared their own longhouse
near to those of their many trainees, which enabled
them to live exactly the same life and forge
closer bonds.

Also included in the training were basic military
disciplines, such as team spirit, mutual depend-
ence, and endurance. Though language presented
difficulties, this was solved with pantomime. This
novel method of communication even extended to
helicopter training without helicopters, throwing
hand-grenades without live grenades, and hand-
to-hand fighting with invisible enemies. These
activities led to both frustration and laughter,
but they certainly worked.

At all times, however, as Sergeant Hunt had
said they should, the men treated the Ibans with
the utmost respect and were particularly rever-
ential to the headman. This even extended to
letting the latter take the salute at Retreat each
evening.

The hearts-and-minds campaign required time and patience but eventually it paid off.

By now the SAS team had its own quarters in a separate longhouse on the edge of the village, from where they were broadcasting daily reports to Squadron Headquarters in Brunei, the 'Haunted House', on a more powerful PRC 320 Clansman radio flown in by Army Air Corps Lieutenant Ralph Ellis.

'You've all lost a lot of weight already,' Ellis noted when they had been there for six weeks.

'The *ulu's* like a fucking steam bath,' Alf replied. 'It just strips a man down.'

This was true. Living in the longhouse for weeks at a time, leaving it only to watch, listen, patrol and report, meant the men were constantly dripping sweat and gasping for air. Even when making the shortest hikes through the jungle, they often found themselves dragging their booted feet laboriously through mud as thick and clinging as quicksand, or wading chest-deep through swamp water covered with sharp, heavy palm leaves and broken branches. These physical demands were in no way eased by the constant strain of trying to look and listen for signs of the enemy, who was known to be able to blend with the *ulu* as well as the animals. Their first two months, then, of living with the Ibans, placed a tremendous physical and mental strain on them, which led to a further loss of weight, in addition to that caused by the oppressive heat and humidity.

'It's fucking tension,' Alf explained, not joking any more. 'It's doing everything for nothing. We yomp through the fucking *ulu*, we wade through the fucking swamps, we get eaten alive by mosquitoes and midges and tormented by flies – and what's it all for? You don't see a thing out there. You hear nothing but the fucking birds. You keep looking over your shoulder for an enemy that isn't there and you start wanting to shoot your best friend just for something to do. Then you come back here. You're stuck in this fucking longhouse. There are more flies and midges and mosquitoes, plus the stench of your own shit and piss coming up through the floorboards. This is life in the raw in the fucking jungle and it's driving me crackers.'

While the hearts-and-minds campaign was not without interest, living on their own just outside the kampong in their own, now crowded, fetid longhouse was both uncomfortable and boring, making each man feel increasingly alienated from himself, forcing him back into his private thoughts and making him dwell on the past.

Being in the jungle reminded Alf of his two trips to Malaya, first in 1953 with the regular Army and then five years later with the SAS. Born in Birkenhead, one of the five children of publicans who worked night and day, Alf felt at home as one of a large group and had therefore taken naturally to the Army. Destined for National Service anyway, he had decided that enlisting would give him certain advantages and, true enough, his first posting overseas, to Butterworth, Malaya, had turned out to be the best experience he had ever had. Depressed when his tour of duty was over, he had signed on for the newly re-formed SAS, gained his winged badge, and soon found himself back in Malaya, this time fighting the communist terrorists in the jungle. Having survived that experience, he was flown back with the others to England, then seconded to the US special forces for advanced medical training in America. He had enjoyed that period, but, for all his moaning, preferred being back in the jungle with his best friend, Pete Welsh, by his side.

Pete was thinking pretty much the same thing. In fact, ever since arriving he had found himself thinking repeatedly of how, when he had first joined the SAS, he had had a chip on his shoulder the size of the Rock of Gibraltar and nearly been thrown out of the regiment because of it. An illegitimate child, he had been raised in London's Finsbury Park by an lone, alcoholic mother who earned her crust as a prostitute and took her revenge out on men by beating her only child, Pete, badly throughout most of his childhood. Joining the Army to escape her, Pete had been trained as an explosives expert and posted to No 101 Special Training School, Singapore. From there he transferred to the 3rd Corps where, with other sappers, he harassed the Japanese by blowing up railways and bridges of strategic importance. He then joined the SAS, and served in Malaya.

Though an excellent soldier, Pete had still got a chip on his shoulder at that time. He only lost it when, in the Telok Anson swamp, actually planning to indirectly kill a fellow trooper who had humiliated him, he realized what he was doing and saved the man's life instead.

Rather like Pete, Dead-eye had joined the Army to escape life at home and had found there a new pride and confidence. Born and bred in West Croydon to a violent lorry driver and a brow-beaten mother, Dead-eye had grown up to be a relatively withdrawn individual, but he had gone even more deeply into himself after witnessing Sergeant Lorrimer's death. Posted to the 2nd Battalion, Royal Regiment of Fusiliers, where his prowess on the firing range soon became a talking point, he realized that he loved being a soldier but wanted an even greater challenge. This led him to apply for a transfer to the SAS when it was re-formed to combat the Emergency in Malaya. He had met Lorrimer there.

Dead-eye had respected Lorrimer more than any other man he had ever known. A veteran of World War Two, a former member of the legendary Long Range Desert Group and the original 1 SAS, also in North Africa, as well as Force 136 – the clandestine resistance unit set up by the British Special Operations Executive (SOE) during World War Two for operations in Japanese-occupied Malaya – then again with the SAS in Malaya during the Emergency, Lorrimer was a legendary old hand who had taught Dead-eye everything he now knew. They had often spent weeks together in the jungle, fighting the CTs with a deadly combination of the Browning autoloader shotgun, the 0.3-inch M1 carbine, No 80 white-phosphorus incendiary hand-grenades, home-made bombs, and even, when silent killing was necessary, with their Fairburn-Sykes commando knives or a crossbow. That had been one of the greatest experiences of Dead-eye's life to date, cementing his friendship with Lorrimer for all time.

Now, in this jungle in Borneo, which was strikingly similar to the jungles of Malaya, Dead-eye was recalling his old friend with particular, deeply wounding clarity. Only work could assuage his pain.

Luckily, the work was plentiful. Once the Gurkhas, Royal Marine Commandos, British Army and other D Squadron, SAS, personnel had moved into the kampong and completed its fortification, the smaller SAS patrols were able to move deeper into the jungle on R & I missions. Eventually, when four villagers who were clearing another landing zone for the SF helicopters were shot by a passing Indonesian or CCO patrol – no evidence of their identity was left behind – which led to the other Ibans becoming more fearful and less cooperative than they had been, Major Callaghan decided to send patrols even deeper into the *ulu* to seek out the enemy and, if necessary, engage with them.

Often augmented by one or two members of the local Police Field Force, these teams made circular tours of the area, some lasting up to five days and including visits to many other kampongs en route. Before moving out, the men painted their weapons with quick-drying green camouflage paint, then wrapped them in strips of cloth specially dyed to match the jungle background and disguise their distinctive shape. In both instances, the men were particularly careful not to let the paint or strips of cloth interfere with the weapons' working parts or sights. After wrapping masking tape around the butts, pistol grips and top covers, they replaced the noisy sling swivels with para-cord, which made no sound at all.

Once the weapons were disguised, they camouflaged themselves, applying 'cam' cream and black 'stick' camouflage to the exposed areas of their skin, including the backs of their hands, and their wrists, ears and neck. The facial camouflage was applied in three stages: first dulling the features with a thin base coating diluted with water (they would use their own saliva when in the jungle); then making diagonal patterns across the face to break up the shape and outline of the features; and finally darkening the areas normally highlighted, such as forehead, nose, cheek bones and chin. To complete this effect, areas normally in shadow were left a lighter shade.

When applying personal camouflage the patrol members paired up to check each other's appearance and ensure that nothing had been missed.

'You look beautiful,' Pete said.

'Not as lovely as you,' Alf said.

'You're just saying that to make me blush, but I think you're sweet anyway.'

'*Terry* looks sweet,' Alf said.

'And he's blushing,' Pete noted. 'Pay a virgin a compliment and she'll blush. It's just one of those things.'

'I'm not blushing,' Terry said.

'Yes, you are,' Pete replied. 'We just can't see it because of the cam cream, but you're blushing, I'll bet.'

'Just shove off,' Terry said.

'He's so bad-tempered,' Alf told Pete, looking deeply, seriously wounded. 'He's a virgin, so you try to be gentle and that's how he behaves. What's the world coming to?'

'Just knock it off,' Terry said. 'Go and look in the mirror and get excited and have a good wank. It's all you're fit for.'

'What a foul mouth!' Alf said.

They moved out on patrol, relieved just to get out, each carrying a bergen packed with enough food and water to last a minimum of five days, each carrying his own personal weapons, including their semi-automatic rifle, commando knife and *parang*, the latter used to hack a path through the dense, often lacerating, undergrowth. Like kampong policemen, they moved on foot. Unlike kampong policemen, they moved unobtrusively, in single file, the lead scout of the patrol followed by the commander and his radio operator, with a gun carrier at the rear playing Tail-end Charlie.

When Dead-eye went out with his three chosen men – Pete, Alf and Terry – as well as three Ibans and five constables from the Police Field Force, they found only signs that some Muruts had been

68

hunting there. Leaving the three tribesmen and the five Police Field Force constables to construct a thatch-and-bamboo observation post overlooking a winding path through the *ulu*, which they suspected was an Indonesian supply route, Dead-eye and his three SAS men tracked down the Muruts just for the practice. A few hours later, they found them in a jungle hide where they were lying up with their blowpipes and dead pigs scattered around them, eating *jarit* and getting drunk on *tapai*. Being friendly, hardworking people who had taken to the British presence in the *ulu*, they invited the SAS men to join them. The subsequent socializing went on for three days, as to leave early would have been impolite. During that time, while the men forced down the vile food and became increasingly light-headed from the alcohol, they picked the brains of the Muruts and learnt a lot about Indonesian and CCO troop movements. Though drunk more often than not, Dead-eye managed to keep his head enough to jot down everything he was hearing.

When, at last, the Muruts moved on, the SAS men felt as if they had been poleaxed. Nevertheless, they made their way back to the rest of the group, who were worried that they had been ambushed by the Indonesians or the CCO.

Returning from the mission, the men, led by Dead-eye, learnt that the threat they had been instilling in the natives was real enough. That very day a force of thirty guerrillas had surrounded the police station at the border town of Tebedu in West Sarawak. After a brisk battle in which a police corporal was killed and two others wounded, the raiders had looted the bazaar. When the news reached the local military HQ, a troop of Royal Marine Commandos was sent to the scene, but the raiders had already disappeared back into the *ulu*, leaving leaflets which stated that the action was a continuation of the earlier revolt in Brunei.

Because of this surprise attack, Major Callaghan ordered all his four-man SAS teams in the area to dig in where they were and await further instructions.

'That's it,' Dead-eye said with no attempt to conceal his pleasure. 'The hearts-and-minds campaign has come to an end. The real war is beginning.'

4

With his SAS patrols dug in over a broad defensive arc, Major Callaghan began sending out more ambitious patrols, trying to track down the infiltrators and put a stop to them. To give Dead-eye more experience, Callaghan placed him in a patrol with Sanderson as his second in command and including Pete Welsh and Alf Laughton, as well as the new man, Terry Malkin, and the same three Ibans they had used before. The patrol was to hike into the high jungle hills of the Pueh Range, which had a peak of nearly 5000 feet and was believed to be a favourite route for CCO agents infiltrating through the jungle to reach Lundu, where the police Special Branch knew a number of communist cells were active.

'Your purpose,' Callaghan informed them, 'is to explore along the mountain range and back down to the lowlands, to locate the CCO forward base used by those terrorists being infiltrated from

Kalimantan. It's in a place called – so the Special Branch believes – Batu Hitam, or Black Rock. A nice, simple job, lads.'

'I'll bet,' Terry murmured.

For this patrol they had to avoid kampongs and any contact with local people, so they carried in their bergens all they might need for two weeks in the *ulu*. This, however, had been limited to 50lb since an excessively heavy bergen in tropical heat could overtax the strength of even an SAS trooper. Their rations would provide only 3500 calories a day (or as little as 2000 for those who chose to make the standard fourteen-day pack last twenty-one days), to save weight in their bergens. Yet to stay fully fit on such active patrols a man needs 5000 calories per day.

'We've lost so much weight already,' Alf observed, 'we'll probably look like ghosts when we get back, after these bloody rations.'

'And nothing from Fortnum and Mason's,' Pete complained. 'That's been reserved for the Ibans.'

'Complain to your squadron commander,' Dead-eye told them. 'Now shut up and let's hump it.'

Before moving out, each man smeared his face and other exposed skin with the usual 'cam' cream and black 'stick' camouflage. Their clothing consisted of a long-sleeved shirt and lightweight trousers tucked into gaiters above standard-issue boots, which had moulded composition soles, cunningly doctored to leave the pattern of an Indonesian, rather than a British, footprint on the jungle floor. They also wore a soft, long-peaked, close-fitting cap or the 'floppy' hat that was stand-ard Army issue, with only a yellow band sewn in the lining as a recognition sign to friendly forces when the hat was put on inside out.

'Just imagine,' Alf said sarcastically. 'You're hiking through the jungle, leaving Indonesian boot marks instead of British, so you're tailed by a couple of your own men. You see them coming up on you, Armalites blazing, so you turn your fucking hat inside out and hope for the best. Some fucking hope!'

Their personal weapons – mainly the 7.62mm Armalite, but with Sanderson carrying his usual 7.62mm SLR and Terry given an M16 5.56mm assault rifle – were also camouflaged with strips of cloth dyed to match the jungle. When Pete held his camouflaged Armalite up to his 'cam'-painted face, the match was perfect.

'The fucking Black and White Minstrel Show,' Alf said. 'Let's all sing *Swanee*!'

Already feeling heavily burdened, Terry was weighed down even more with the PRC 320 Clansman radio, weighing 11 1/2lb, which he carried on his back, allowing him the use of both arms. The Clansman had a hand generator system, an alternate, or emergency, rechargeable nickel-cadmium battery, and a sky-wave facility of 30–1200 miles, with a ground-wave range of over 25 miles. It could also be operated by remote control from a distance of up to two miles.

'That's a damned good radio,' Pete told Terry, 'if a bit on the heavy side.'

'Right,' Terry said.

'The last man we had humping that fucking thing,' Alf contributed, 'collapsed after a four-hour hike with a heart attack. Went down like a log, he did.'

'Thanks a lot,' Terry said.

'He was older than you, though,' Pete said.

'By two years,' Alf added.

'Won a silver cup for running,' Pete said, 'but that bloody radio did him in.'

'If I'd wanted Morecambe and Wise,' Terry said, 'I'd have asked the BBC. Let's just call it a day, guys.'

'Such spirit!' Alf sang.

The patrol was escorted by five Police Field Force scouts as far as the border, which ran north–south along the mountain ridge. There the men moved out on their own, striking west from the border, heading into Indonesian jungle where they could as easily be ambushed as ambush an Indonesian patrol.

Within minutes of hiking into the dense jungle of the mountain range, Terry again experienced that oppressive awareness of vast silence combined with a chilling absence of colour and light. Mercifully, as they were already high in the hills, they had no swamps to brave, but almost as frightening to him were the many aerial walkways that swayed in the wind high above the gorges where, in the dizzying depths, streams wound, often violently over sharp rocks, between the high, muddy walls.

The aerial walkways were like miniature suspension bridges, but made of bamboo instead of steel. The walkway itself was constructed from only three lengths of thick bamboo, wide enough to span the gorge and laid down side by side to form a dangerously narrow path. The gaps in the bamboo uprights on either side of the walkway were three to four feet wide, with other lengths of bamboo running along them to be used as handrails.

Treading along the walkway, holding onto to the bamboo handrails on either side, a man was exposed to the full force of the wind blowing along the gorge. This was only made worse by the wide spaces between the uprights, which forced him to look down on the frightening, dizzying drop on either side. Nor could he ignore the constant, sickening swaying of the wind-blown walkway, often suspended a good hundred feet or more above the torrential river sweeping through the narrow gorge on a bed of sharp stones. There was no way to survive such a fall and all the men knew it.

Crossing the walkways was a stomach-churning experience and there were many to cross in the mountain range. Immensely relieved each time they stepped off a creaking, swaying aerial walkway, the men were then faced with yet another steep climb through the dense, often impenetrable undergrowth on the face of the steep hills. Their aching, forward advance often involved hacking away the undergrowth with their *parangs*, a task rendered even more difficult and dangerous by the steep fall of the hills, the loose soil underfoot and the lack of something to cling to if they slipped, since many of the branches were covered with sharp spikes and razor-edged palm leaves. The men therefore often slipped back, even fell and rolled down, while desperately trying to keep the blade of the *parang* away from their face and hands as they reached desperately for a hold on something that would stop them from rolling further.

All of this was made even more frustrating by the almost suffocating humidity, the sweat dripping constantly in their eyes, and the usual swarms of bloated flies and mosquitoes which frenziedly tried to feed off the sweat. They were also faced with a disturbing number of snakes, some venomous, which slept coiled around branches or slithered across the jungle paths, often hidden under the leaves on the ground, appearing as long, narrow mounds that moved magically forward while curving sinuously from left to right. Also, spiders and stinging ants often fell on them when the branches of trees were shaken accidentally.

'Christ!' Terry hissed, breathing heavily, when something large and hairy fell on him and bounced off his shoulder. 'That bastard was as big as my fist!'

'It was only a tarantula,' Pete replied. 'Its bark is worse than its bite.'

'It's the bleedin' *ants* that have the bite,' Terry said, 'and I'm black and blue.'

'No more talking from this moment on,' Deadeye told them, 'unless it's absolutely necessary. This is a silent patrol.'

Terry shivered, remembering the enormous spider, then he filled up with gloom at the prospect of not being able to break the suffocating silence of the jungle with conversation. Nevertheless, he moved on with the others, his face, shirt and trousers soaked with sweat.

Their routine was to march for an hour before

breakfast, which consisted of dried biscuits and tinned sardines, washed down with water. The water was usually drawn from a fast-flowing stream. If taken from a pool or slow-flowing stream, it would be purified with dissolving tablets before being used. Dead-eye would not even permit them to brew tea in case the smoke gave away their position.

For lunch they might have a few more biscuits and a tin of cheese, keeping the meatier items in their ration packs for supper just before nightfall.

Dead-eye permitted no cooking on this patrol. Though they might go cold and hungry, he explained, they were definitely a lot safer not attracting the attention of an Indonesian patrol, or even the region's headhunting Land Dyaks, to the sight of camp-fire smoke or the smells of cooking.

Halting either for a short break on the march or for one of their three miserable meals of the day, the men sat on their bergens, resting their rifles across their laps or cradling them in their crooked arms, either way always alert. If they talked, it was only to exchange brief sentences in a whisper. Meanwhile, as scout Dead-eye scanned the jungle ahead, while the navigator, the more experienced Sanderson, rechecked his route with a combination of map, magnifying glass and compass. The rest periods were therefore not all that restful and by last light all the men were exhausted.

After the draining heat and humidity of the day, the high mountain range could be surprisingly cold at night. Their lying-up positions, or LUPs, consisted mainly of uncovered shallow 'scrapes' in which they unrolled their hollow-fill sleeping bags on plastic sheeting. Above these simple bedding arrangements they raised a shelter consisting of a waterproof poncho draped over wire stretched taut between two Y-shaped sticks, making a triangular tent with the apex pointing into the wind. Sometimes, if camping out beneath the trees, they would construct a fresh-leaf shelter consisting of a low framework with a sloping roof. After collecting the largest leaves available, they thatched them into the bamboo framework of the roof. The four sides were made from bamboo and thatch woven together and lashed firmly in place with rattan vines. They then made a huge pile of branches and leaves as a mattress, put on all their clothes, smeared themselves with mud, if available, to keep away the insects, and finally covered themselves with groundsheets. Though taking longer to make, the fresh-leaf shelter afforded more protection than one made from a poncho.

Before moving on the next morning, just before first light, they meticulously removed all signs of their overnight bivvies. Even branches and leaves that had been disturbed were pushed back into their natural positions. This was a tedious, but vitally necessary routine.

As they moved further west, cresting the summit of the mountain range, exploring along it, then circling back down to lower ground, the need to be alert to a chance meeting with a Land Dyak became more pronounced. The Land Dyaks were not familiar with white men and tended to be suspicious of all strangers, including the Ibans from the coastal areas, such as the three travelling with the SAS patrol. Given that they were skilled at jungle warfare and still practised headhunting, they were a breed of native best avoided.

As Sanderson helpfully informed the rest of the group, smiling only slightly, the Land Dyaks were likely to come out of the wilder jungle heading towards the settlements along the Sempayang River, where there were many paddy-fields (as distinct from dry *padi* fields) for the growing of rice in traditional watery beds. The men saw the paddy-fields soon enough when they reached the lower slopes and began their sweaty hike along the river. The crops of seedlings, which would not be harvested until April, gave no cover, so the patrol kept mainly to a jungle-covered spur from which there was a view of the river.

In the event, the only Land Dyak they met was one they saw ankle-deep in the river, fishing with a blowpipe and darts smeared with a substance that paralysed the fish without leaving poison in its system.

Leaving the rest of his group hiding in the shelter of the trees, Dead-eye sneaked up on the tribesman, aimed his Armalite at him, and called out in Malay for him to turn around. Startled, the man did so, then studied Dead-eye with a gaze more considered than afraid. He did not put his hands up – the gesture was probably unknown to him – but simply stood there, holding the blowpipe by his side, staring at Dead-eye as if studying some new breed of animal.

'You are stranger,' he said, speaking in Malay.

'Yes,' Dead-eye replied, still aiming his weapon at the long-haired, half-naked native and keeping his eye on the blowpipe. 'I am a visitor here and wish you no harm. I look for the Indonesian soldiers. Have you seen any?'

The tribesman nodded and pointed along the river with his blowpipe. 'Batu Hitam,' he said.

'Anywhere else?' Dead-eye asked.

The Dyak shook his head from side to side, indicating no.

'And Batu Hitam is straight along the river?'

This time the Dyak nodded, again without speaking. He then pointed upriver.

'Thank you,' Dead-eye said, then backed away to where the rest of his group were hidden, crouched low at the edge of the *ulu*. He did not remove his gaze from the Dyak's blowpipe, but by the time he reached the shelter of trees, the native had already returned to his work, blowing his poisoned darts into the water, then reaching down to snatch up the immobilized fish.

'Learn anything?' Sanderson asked.

'Only that the Indos are in Batu Hitam, further upriver. He says he hasn't seen them anywhere else.'

'Then let's head upriver,' Sanderson said, 'and find their camp.'

'Right, men,' Dead-eye said, glancing at the others. 'Let's haul out.'

Heading upriver, sticking close to the bank, they reached Batu Hitam in two hours. There, from where they were hiding at the edge of the forest, they saw a Dyak settlement, clearly filled with headhunters, judging from the number of shrunken skulls strung over the doors of the thatched longhouses. But there was no trace of the Indonesians. Circling around the settlement, crouched low, weapons at the ready, taking note of the fact that the male Dyaks were armed with spears and blowpipes, they carefully checked every aspect of the village, but still saw no sign of either Indonesian soldiers or the CCO.

Just as they were about to turn back, however, one of the Iban trackers, Ejok, raised and lowered his clenched right fist repeatedly, indicating that the rest of the patrol should join him. When they did so, he showed them a lot of footprints in the swampy ground near the river, leading from the settlement to the river bank. All the footprints were of men who had been wearing Indonesian jungle boots.

'They must have been here,' Ejok said in Malay, nodding back in the direction of the settlement. 'These bootprints are fresh, so they must have left only recently, maybe this morning, taking boats from here and heading upriver. As they have left no sign of their presence in the camp, they don't intend coming back.'

'Damn!' Dead-eye said softly.

Sanderson sighed. 'We've lost them. We're not allowed to stay out longer than two weeks. We'll have to go back empty-handed.'

Dead-eye was visibly frustrated. He ordered the patrol to turn around and go back downstream. They crossed the river two hours later, just before reaching the spot where the Dyak had been fishing, then they began the long hike to the forward operating base, three days' 'tab' away.

During that sweaty, exhausting hike they lost even more weight when, wading chest-deep through the swamps of the humid lowland forests, they were covered in leeches that greedily fed off them. By the time they had reached dry land again, where they could burn them off, they had all lost a lot of blood, as well as more weight.

On reaching the FOB, still without having made contact with the enemy, let alone a sighting of them, they were even more frustrated to learn that another SAS-led patrol had successfully ambushed a Chinese party on the mountain six miles west of the Bemban where an Indonesian base was known to be located. A second patrol had found a deserted Indonesian fort with mortar pits and well-sited defences. A third patrol, waiting to ambush a CCO patrol, had themselves been attacked by a 100-strong Indonesian platoon on the Bemban track. The SAS men suffered no casualties and managed to kill at least eleven of them before making a quick withdrawal.

'We're the only ones who saw and did nothing,' Dead-eye said bitterly. 'What a waste of time!'

'Everything comes to him who waits,' Major Callaghan replied with a teasing grin. 'Now go and get some sleep, Dead-eye.'

Dead-eye joined the others back in the spider, where he slept like a log.

5

'In the words of our commanding officer,' Major Callaghan said in the briefing room of the Haunted House, 'this is the year that began with the end of a revolution and ended with the beginning of an undeclared war.'

Pausing to let those words sink in, he wiped sweat from his forehead and waved flies away from his face. A large fan whirred above his head.

'That undeclared war has commenced along the frontier,' he continued, 'so you men will be moved back to the unmapped mountain border of Sarawak – the so-called 'Gap' – also known as the 3rd Division. You will concentrate your efforts on the shorter frontier between Indonesia and Brunei, which has chosen to remain a British Protectorate rather than join the new Federation. There you will engage in aggressive raids into enemy territory.'

The men sitting in rows of hard-backed wooden chairs under two more large rotating fans cheered and applauded. Callaghan waited for them to settle down before he continued.

'The object of the raids is to pre-empt any likely Indonesian build-up or attack; to harass the Indonesians on patrol and in their camps; and to gradually compel them to move their forces away from the border. As the major purpose, then, is to deter or thwart aggression by the Indonesians, no attacks will be mounted in retribution or with the sole aim of damaging the enemy. The enemy is only to be engaged as a last defensive resort. Where this is the case, minimum force should be used, rather than large-scale attacks, to avoid escalation.'

Seeing the expression on the faces of his men, Callaghan felt a certain regret. It was obvious from their faces that they were delighted to be back in action; and Callaghan, who himself liked nothing better than action, wanted to go with them. Unfortunately, as Squadron Commander, he was going to be kept back at HQ, mapping out the campaign, analysing the intelligence, and controlling the various patrols by radio based on that information. It was an exciting job in its own way, but not quite what he wanted.

'Collectively, the raids will be known as "Claret" operations and classified "Top Secret",' he told them. 'Initial penetration distance into Indonesian territory will be 5000 yards, though this may be extended to 20,000.'

'I could piss 5000 yards,' Alf said. 'It's not worth considering.'

'Yes, it is,' Callaghan said firmly when the laughter had died down. 'Your primary function will be deep penetration and the gathering of intelligence across enemy lines, engaging the enemy if necessary.' The latter part of that remark raised a few more cheers. 'This penetration will include the river routes used by the Indonesians as military supply routes, to move men and equipment up to the border. You will count the boats and the men on those MSRs, and map suitable areas from which they can be ambushed from the river bank. Last but not least, you'll locate the kampongs and bases from which the boats are coming and, if at all possible, enter them without alerting the sentries or dogs, recce them, then slip back out into the jungle.'

'Sounds better than suffering the horrors of *jarit* and *tapai* in order to win hearts and minds,' Pete said tartly. 'Count me in, boss.'

'It's *because* you drink *tapai*,' Alf told him, 'that you can fart from your mouth. Can we get on with the briefing, thanks?'

'OK, men, let's dampen it.' Though smiling, Callaghan sounded serious, so the men quietened down again. 'The first cross-border patrols,' the major informed them, 'will be made by two- to five-man teams *not* accompanied by local guides. You'll carry exactly the same equipment and weapons as you've used in Sarawak, with the main small arm being the Armalite rifle.'

'Why the Armalite?'

'It's presently viewed as the perfect jungle weapon, being portable and powerful. Also, though used widely around the world, it isn't standard issue to the British Army. Therefore, if wounded or taken prisoner, you can attribute your presence in Indonesian territory to a map-reading error, which should sound, in the circumstances, reasonably plausible.'

'It might if we're caught on the river banks,' Dead-eye pointed out. 'But it certainly won't if we're caught near their kampongs or training bases.'

Callaghan sighed. 'No, I'm afraid that in those circumstances you won't have a leg to stand on and will be treated rather harshly by your captors.'

'The understatement of the year,' Alf said.

'Fat chance of *me* being caught,' Pete added.

'Don't treat the possibility lightly,' Callaghan warned him. 'Having already been out there, the 1st/2nd Gurkha Company has discovered that a lot of the approach tracks to the camps and kampongs are mined. Also, outlying machine-gun positions add considerably to the overall camp defences.'

'I'll piss on them from 5000 yards,' Alf said, 'and put out their fire.'

'I wouldn't call him a boastful man,' Pete said, 'but there are those who are humbler.'

'How do we navigate?' Dead-eye asked in a sombre tone when further ribald remarks had faded away.

Callaghan was prompt and precise in his response. 'Through the scrutiny of air photographs; cultivation of a photographic memory of topographical features such as rivers and ridges, as well as their compass bearings; and a precise sense of distance walked to calculate a dead reckoning of mileage covered by reference to time-on-march. You will also use jungle tracking as a means of following the enemy to their kampongs or bases.'

'How do we engage?' Dead-eye asked, getting to the heart of the matter.

'Mainly the shoot-and-scoot standard operating procedure.' This meant breaking contact with the enemy as soon as possible, whenever contact occurred, and making themselves scarce again, disappearing like ghosts. Some of the men groaned aloud when they heard this approach proposed, voicing their disapproval, but Callaghan waved them into silence. 'I know this particular SOP isn't popular with many of you, but it's our belief that it'll keep casualties to a minimum, while simultaneously disorientating the enemy. I know you'd rather stay and fight it out, but shoot-and-scoot it will have to be.'

'Whoever devised that SOP,' Pete said, 'should be hung, drawn and quartered.'

'I devised it in Malaya,' Callaghan responded, 'with your old friend Sergeant Lorrimer.' He waited for the embarrassed silence to grip the room, then moved in for the kill. 'It's already proved its effectiveness more than once, in circumstances similar to the ones you'll soon find yourselves in, so while your moans and groans are acceptable, don't try refusing.'

'No, boss!' Alf said, knowing when he was beaten.

Now confident that he had the upper hand, Callaghan smiled again – a merciless smile – as he gave them even worse news. 'Please bear in mind, also, that if you get lost, or are captured, no rescue will be attempted by the other men in your patrol.' When he felt that they had digested this harsh fact, he explained: 'Nothing is to be left in enemy territory that will betray our presence there. No casualties, dead or wounded, to be left behind. No identity discs, photos or letters from home. No cigarette stubs. No spent cartridge cases.

Not even the prints of your boots. Regarding the latter, you will be asked to wear irregular footwear, with sacking or hessian over your boots, shoes and sandals to blur all marks indicating their origin. You will check every leaf and spider's web, leaving absolutely no trace of your movements. Any questions so far?'

Corporal Sanderson put up his hand. 'How long will the individual raids last?'

'Approximately three weeks each.' Someone gave a low whistle of surprise. 'Yes,' Callaghan said, 'it's a long time. And as you'll be obliged to live on dehydrated rations based on a relatively meagre 3500 calories per day instead of the recommended minimum of 5000, you can expect to lose a considerable amount of weight.'

'We've already lost that,' Terry informed him.

'You're going to lose even more,' Callaghan responded bluntly. 'On your return, *if* you return, you'll have a one-day debriefing, followed by a two-day period of total rest, then a two-day briefing for the next patrol. You move out again after a total of five days back here, during which time you should have put your lost weight back on.'

'Only to lose it again on the next patrol,' Sergeant Hunt said sardonically from the back of the room.

'Given your impressive paunch, Sergeant, I don't think it will harm you.'

91

The men had a good laugh at that, but Hunt took it in good part. 'What about air support?' he asked when the laughter had died away.

'It will only be given in cases of extreme emergency. Otherwise, forget it.'

Callaghan glanced left and right, from one row of faces to the other, trying to glance at each trooper in turn, even if only for a few seconds. 'Any more questions?' When most of the men shook their heads, Callaghan nodded.

'Some points to note,' he said, wrapping it up. 'For these particular raids, the important thing is not how much you can carry, but how far you can travel with the minimum of equipment. You can't go head down, arse up in this kind of situation, so prior to your departure we'll be weighing your bergens to check that they're not a single ounce over the maximum weight of 50lb. If they are, certain items will be taken out, no matter how much you value them, until the weight is reduced to the permitted level.' He ignored the groans of disgust. 'Also, between now and when you leave, your NCOs will be making random urine and blood tests to ensure that you're all taking your Paludrine against malaria. I don't care if you wash them down with beer, but make sure you take them.' He grinned at the rolling eyes and murmurs of protest. When these had subsided, he raised his hands, calling for complete silence. 'All right, gentlemen, I think I've had my turn. Now it's yours. Good day and good luck.'

The men applauded him unreservedly.

6

The first cross-border raids were tentative probes over the ridge into Indonesian territory by unaccompanied groups of between two and five men carrying exactly the same equipment and weapons they had used before. The same team that had made the unproductive hike to Batu Hitam, still under the command of Dead-eye with Corporal Sanderson as his second in command, was given the task of reaching the River Koemba, which ran for three miles parallel to the border of western Sarawak.

'This border from Cape Datu in the north,' Captain Callaghan explained to Dead-eye in his private office in the Haunted House, 'crosses the coastal plain where Gurkhas and Royal Marines of the Special Boat Squadron have patrolled from time to time. It then runs north–south along the Pueh Range,' he continued, tracing a line with his forefinger on the map spread out on his desk, 'and turns south-eastwards across the flat lands north of the Sentimo marshes.' He tapped the marked area with his forefinger, looking rather distracted. 'Here the Sarawak border runs across trading tracks leading to Stass. The only major routes crossing the border for the next 30 miles of frontier run along mountain ridges north of the Koemba and further eastwards parallel to the Sentimo marshes.'

'So, the obvious, if not necessarily easy, crossing for any Indonesian invasion,' Dead-eye replied, looking down at the map, 'is still through Stass and on to the Sarawak capital of Kuching.'

'Exactly,' Callaghan said, always pleased by Dead-eye's quick, intuitive grasp of military strategy. 'So that's where we want you to cause your little disruptions.'

'No problem,' Dead-eye said.

'Unfortunately, there *is* a problem. SAS patrols sent out earlier this year reached the edge of the Sentimo marshes and the headwaters of the Koemba, but were unable to penetrate the marshes north of the river. You might come to the same grief.'

In fact, Dead-eye's group did. They spent over a week trying to reach the upper part of the river and the mountain plateau separating it from the Sentimo marshes. This involved hiking through dense primary and secondary jungle. In the latter, known as *belukar*, the foliage had been cleared and was growing back again, thicker than ever, to form an often impenetrable tangle of palms, tree-ferns, bracken, seedling trees, rattans and other sharp thorns. Here, too, the moss-covered tree trunks often soared to over 100 feet, wrapped in another tangle of huge leaves, thick creepers and liana, forming an almost solid canopy above which blotted out the sun. Because of this lack of light the ground was wet and often slippery with mud, making progress slow and dirty; it also reminded the already struggling men that the actual swamps could not be far away.

This turned out to be true. Finally emerging from a gruelling struggle through a stretch of *belukar*, the men found themselves faced with primary jungle filled with large swamps. These were hell to cross. The muddy water often came up to the waist, and sometimes the chest. It was covered with drifting debris, including large, razor-sharp leaves, thorny brambles, broken branches, seedlings, and spiders' webs succumbing to the slime. This debris was in turn covered with dark swarms of flies and mosquitoes that buzzed and whined frantically around the men, covering their unprotected eyes, lips and noses. The men were further tormented by this because they could do nothing to prevent it, being forced to hold their weapons above their heads while trying to feel their way with their booted feet over an underwater bed rendered treacherous by shifting mud, tangled weeds, sharp or rolling stones, thorny branches that also moved when stepped on, and unexpected holes that could trap the feet.

Nor could the troopers prevent themselves being covered by the slimy, worm-like leeches that crawled onto them from wet vegetation and sucked their blood as they waded through the swamp holding their weapons aloft. But even more tormenting was the fact that in many areas of the swamps the lower branches of the trees stretched out across the water, often practically touching it, forcing the men to either work their way around them, which could double the distance travelled, or duck under them. This latter course of action presented the risk of being cut by thorns and sharp palm leaves or, even worse, could cause them to accidentally shake more leeches, poisonous snakes or spiders off their wet leaves, branches or glistening webs filled with trapped insects.

In fact, one of the main dangers of wading through the water was the possibility of an encounter with venomous sea snakes, which had flattened, paddle-shaped tails and, being the same brownish colour as the broken branches, could easily be mistaken for them until it was too late. Luckily, no one was attacked.

Nevertheless, it took a few more days to make it through the swamps and marshes, which meant that they had to sleep there as well. Sometimes, if they were lucky, they could sling hammocks between tree trunks. But when this was not possible they were forced to sleep standing upright, often waist-deep in water, usually tying themselves to a tree trunk to prevent themselves falling over. While acutely uncomfortable, this did allow them a little sleep, though it was rarely deep or truly restorative.

If the jungle's silence was oppressive during the day, by night it gave way to an eerie cacophony of croaking, hissing, flapping, snapping, rustling, squawking, buzzing and whining that penetrated the senses of those sleeping and frequently jerked them awake. To this kind of disruption of normal sleep was added their own fear, which also kept them awake, of slipping out of their ropes and sinking into the water, too tired to realize what was happening before they drowned; or of being bitten by venomous snakes or eels while their bodies sagged in the water. The leeches fed off their blood all night, but this no longer concerned them.

Finally, after five days of such horrors, already exhausted and only halfway through the patrol, the men reached the upper part of the river – only to find that the sheer cliffs of the plateau offered no possible route to the jungle over 800 feet below, on the other side of the mountain range.

They had to turn back.

To make matters worse, on their return journey across the border, through the hellish swamps, then the dense *belukar*, and finally the dark, humid primary jungle leading to the rendezvous point, they almost shot up some of their own men, when, hiding at night in the jungle, they heard what they could only assume was an Indonesian or CCO patrol coming along the path they were overlooking.

Immediately they dropped low and took aim with their Armalites, preparing to open fire. The first 'enemy' troops appeared around a bend in the path, not attempting to hide themselves, and only when Dead-eye recognized the 0.3-inch M1 carbines they were carrying did he realize that they were actually a patrol of Dyak Border Scouts, coming to meet up at the wrong RV.

'Don't fire!' Dead-eye bawled instantly, then he leapt out upon the startled Dyaks, some of whom nearly opened fire at the sight of him. After an acrimonious exchange, Dead-eye's group joined the confused tribesmen on the short hike back through the darkness to their correct RV.

Frustrated by the failure of his SAS groups to get beyond the Sentimo marshes and still constrained by not being permitted to use them for overtly aggressive actions, Major Callaghan revised his strategy and, instead, concentrated on planning offensive cross-border operations by the Gurkha battalions, with the SAS acting as scouts.

While this still led to a certain amount of frustration for some of the SAS men, notably those such as Dead-eye, they all conceded that it was better than doing nothing and could even be quite relaxing, particularly after the relative isolation of the earlier patrols, which had emotionally drained many of them.

Terry Malkin was one of those convinced that scouting for the Gurkha battalions was almost pleasant when compared to the R & I patrols through the *ulu*, when the silence and gloom, combined with the frightening isolation of the five-man team, had given him more than one bad night.

Not that the scouting work was not demanding, both physically and mentally. Certainly, in the windless, silent days in the jungle, being a scout had its own difficulties and discomforts. For instance, no trooper was allowed to eat, smoke or unscrew his water bottle without his platoon commander's permission. At night, sentries checked any man who snored or talked in his sleep. Whenever the company was on the move, a recce section led the way, their packs carried by the SAS men behind. Because of the long approach march, each man carried six days' basic rations together with various lightweight additions and a small reserve in a belt pouch, but these were barely sufficient for his needs.

Nevertheless, even more demanding than the marches were the many periods when the scouts had to remain stationary to watch and listen for the enemy.

As Dead-eye explained to Terry when he had complained about such stops: 'The man who's stationary in the jungle has the tactical advantage. Not moving himself, making no sound of his own, he can see and hear a lot more of the enemy movements. That gives him the upper hand.'

It was for that reason, therefore, that the SAS scouts were compelled to spend as much as twenty minutes in every half hour sitting and listening, only marching during the other ten minutes. It made for slow, frustrating progress, but it kept them alive.

Nevertheless, if scouting for the Gurkha battalions had its own share of danger, tension, isolation and frustration, Terry noticed the difference in the evening when, having completed the day's recce in the *ulu*, he could return, not to a tiny, cramped jungle hide with his small, relatively defenceless team, but to a whole battalion of Gurkhas in their camp. This tended to make him feel a lot safer and, in many ways, more human. It was a good feeling to be in the middle of their perimeter, warmed by a camp-fire, eating decent food, and surrounded by so many small, cheerful, brown-faced men, whom he knew were actually ferocious fighters. To see them at night in their sangars, spaced evenly around the perimeter, with their GPMGs aiming out in all directions, made the novice SAS man feel safe.

He even felt safer than normal when, just before he was due to return with the rest of Dead-eye's team, the SAS led the Gurkhas to an Indonesian camp they had found recently. To reach the camp, they had to hike through the night, arriving just after dawn.

Completely surrounded by thick undergrowth, the camp consisted of a few thatched huts on stilts, some open latrines covered with clouds of flies, and a protective ring of sunken gun emplacements and defensive trenches. The Indonesian soldiers were seated in large groups around smoking open fires, breakfasting on roast pig, when the Gurkhas arrived and spread out in a great circle around the camp, though remaining well hidden in the forest. In that same thick undergrowth, the Gurkhas and

SAS men quietly brought into position British 3-inch mortars, Soviet RPG-7 rocket launchers, M79 single-shot, breech-loading grenade-launchers, and GPMGs and Bren light machine-guns. The gun and mortar teams were in touch with one another through their small, backpacked A41 radio sets and, at the command from the Gurkha commander, they would fire simultaneously.

Kneeling in the darkness with Pete and Alf on one side of him and the inscrutable Dead-eye on the other, Terry, as signaller, was listening to his A41 with a racing heart and sweat on his brow. Though five years in the Irish Guards, he had not actually seen combat before, and realized that at last he was about to take part in a fire-fight. Any advances to be made would, he knew, be made by the Gurkhas, with the SAS giving covering fire; but that in itself was close enough to the real thing to make him feel simultaneously nervous and excited. He would be, after all, in the line of enemy fire and therefore in considerable danger. Yes, this *was* the real thing.

Glancing to the left, past Dead-eye's granite profile, Terry saw the Gurkha commander raise his clenched fist, preparing to give the order to fire. Glancing back at the enemy camp, he saw the many soldiers in their jungle-greens still squatting around the open fires, waving smoke from their faces, eating roast pork and rice, laughing, joking and relaxing as if they had all the time in the world. They were inside the perimeter. Around the perimeter in the sunken gun emplacements, the sentries were, in many instances, also paying more attention to food and drink than they were to what was happening in the jungle.

Terry studied them intently. They seemed very unconcerned. He was in a trance of watchfulness, studying the soldiers around the fires, when the voice of the Gurkha commander snapped 'Open fire!' in Malay, his voice reverberating eerily in Terry's headset, followed almost simultaneously by the crump-crump of mortars and the sudden, savage roar of the combined rocket-launchers and machine-guns.

Even before Terry had quite grasped what was happening, the first mortar shells were exploding in and between the gun emplacements and defensive trenches, as well as among the Indonesians around the camp-fires. At the same time, a barrage of 2.25kg missiles, 40mm fin-stabilized grenades and 7.62mm tracer bullets was flaring across the clearing and disappearing into the flames and boiling smoke caused by the first mortar explosions.

Some gun emplacements and slit trenches were destroyed instantly in violent eruptions of spewing soil, with broken bodies hurled upwards and out like burning rag dolls; but others returned the fire, their guns spitting fire and smoke, causing different-coloured tracers to race outwards from the perimeter and into the jungle.

One of the huts inside the camp exploded in flames as the jungle around Terry went wild, with shells and tracers zipping past on both sides and foliage being blown to shreds all around him.

'Open fire!' Dead-eye bawled.

Just about to hug the ground to avoid the return fire of the enemy, Terry instead found himself firing his Armalite at the men jumping up from their camp-fires, grabbing their weapons and running left and right to find cover as the huts blazed behind them and more shells and bullets cut them to pieces.

Another hut exploded, disintegrating in a ball of fire, with the men nearby, also on fire, hurled in all directions. Within seconds the camp had been obscured in a grim pall of smoke through which shadowy figures and brighter flames could just about be discerned; though the screams of the wounded and dying actually rose above the deafening bedlam of the roaring guns and explosions.

Terry kept firing, feeling as if he was dreaming but vividly aware of the return fire flashing and snapping angrily on both sides, kicking up the soil in front of him, then blowing apart the foliage directly above to make it rain down on him. He kept his finger on the trigger until the magazine was empty, ejected it, loaded another, and continued to fire at the shadowy figures running and falling in that hellish tapestry of flame and smoke.

He did not know if the men falling in his sights had been hit by him or by some of those firing methodically around him; nor did he care. He just could not stop. The men around him also continued firing with everything they had – mortars, rocket launchers, machine-guns, sub-machine-guns and rifles – until the return fire from the enemy camp had diminished considerably and, eventually, started to taper off altogether.

Terry was not sure if he had heard the second command on his headset or not, but suddenly, as the smoke cleared, two assault platoons of Gurkhas moved in to clear the camp, advancing at the crouch, firing on the move, and not stopping to take prisoners or ask questions.

'Selective firing only,' Dead-eye ordered, switching to single-shot and starting to give selective covering fire by picking off individuals who looked like being a threat to the advancing Gurkhas. 'We want no own goals,' he added, meaning that they were not to accidentally shoot any of their own men, in this case the Gurkhas. 'Do it right or stop firing.'

Terry did not stop firing. Now, for the first time,

with the smoke clearing and the enemy thinning, he knew exactly which falling men had been shot by him and felt better about it. It was an odd, uncomfortable feeling, perhaps even shameful, but it filled him with an odd kind of pride as well – odd because tinged with fear.

Though most of the soldiers in and around the camp had been put out of action, either dead or seriously wounded, a number of naked, panic-stricken Indonesians suddenly rushed out from around the burning ruins of a hut demolished by mortar fire. Not waiting to find out if they had arms or booby-traps behind their backs, the ferocious little Gurkhas dealt with them quickly and ruthlessly, cutting them down in a hail of fire from their SLRs and M16s. When the last of the naked men had fallen, all resistance ended.

'Cease fire,' Dead-eye said to the men beside him.

Standing up beside the impassive Dead-eye and his two more excited corporals, Terry saw that most of the enemy gun emplacements and defensive trenches were now blackened shell holes, that most of the camp-fires had been blown apart by gunfire, that all of the huts hit by the mortars were either still blazing or smouldering, and that the dead and wounded were scattered all around the clearing in an unholy mess of other shell holes, spent shells, buckled weapons, shreds of clothing, dismembered limbs and spreading pools of blood. Turning away from that ghastly sight, he met the fathomless grey gaze of Sergeant Parker.

'You did pretty good,' Dead-eye told him. 'You've just earned your winged dagger.'

Young Terry was too numb to respond.

'You'll recover,' Dead-eye said.

7

Terry recovered. Six weeks later he was kneeling with the other members of a five-man group that included another new man, Trooper Kenneth Burgess, Welsh Guards, in the dense foliage at the side of a jungle track known to be used as an Indonesian military supply route. This was at the tail end of a four-week period in which many small groups of SAS men, having finally received formal approval to do more than 'watch and count' or act as scouts for the Gurkhas, had broadened the scope of the 'Claret' raids to include attacks on enemy approach routes and MSRs, either by road or water, ambushing tracks and rivers, and setting booby-traps where it was known that the Indonesian or CCO raiders would pass. The range of penetration across the border had therefore been greatly increased and the pre-emptive actions undertaken by the unaccompanied SAS groups had increased in both frequency and ferocity.

Basing most of their attack methods on Major Callaghan's 'shoot-and-scoot' SOP, the groups had made the essence of their ambushes speed of movement and reaction: hitting the enemy from close range with a brief, savage fusillade of small-arms fire, including hand-grenades, then vanishing speedily, leaving the counter-attackers to find nothing but apparently empty jungle. These tactics were highly successful, causing a lot of damage, and soon the SAS were getting tales back from the Dyaks and other aboriginals about how the Indonesians and CCO were whispering fearful stories about their 'invisible' attackers.

For this reason the SAS troopers started calling themselves the 'Tiptoe Boys'.

At other times, however, the attacks would be lengthier, more sophisticated affairs with electronically detonated Claymore mines catching an enemy's front and rear, while the SAS troopers' automatic fire raked the centre.

Which is what Terry's group were planning this very minute, as their last and largest attack before heading back to the RV. So, while Terry, Dead-eye and Alf knelt in the firing position in the shadow of the trees by the side of the road, spaced well apart to give a broad arc of fire, their demolition expert, Pete Welsh, quickly and expertly laid his four Claymores approximately equidistant along the centre of a 100-yard stretch of road, placed so as to catch the front and rear of the Indonesian column, as well as the middle.

Invented by the Germans during World War Two, the Claymore anti-tank mine consists of a round, flattish dish with a concave plate of steel on its face. It is filled with explosive. When detonated, the plate is blown off and can go through the side or front of a Panther tank at a distance of 80 yards. After the war the Americans modified the Claymore to fire metal spikes, or 'slugs', instead of the plate. When this modified Claymore is exploded, its 350 razor-sharp slugs will fly out over a sixty-degree arc to a range of 100 yards, shredding anyone unfortunate enough to be within its range. It is a terrible weapon.

Pete was wiring his Claymores for detonation by remote control. This enabled him to bury them in the ground, face up, resting on their spiked base, with earth and leaves thrown over them to disguise their presence.

As he watched Pete lay the Claymores and, at the same time, kept his ear cocked for the sound of advancing Indonesians, Terry thought with pride of the many attacks he had made with this small group since his baptism of fire with the Gurkhas near the River Koemba. Though not exactly frightened by that attack, he had been shocked by the results of it, dwelling for days on the carnage it had caused. Nevertheless, as Dead-eye had promised him, he had recovered soon enough and gone on to his other fire-fights with more confidence and a necessary pragmatism. Distancing himself from the bloody results of what he was engaged in, he had learned to treat it as a job, in a professional manner, and eventually, after three or four more attacks with this five-man team, had even started taking pride in a job well done.

Luckily, their personal attacks had so far been uniformly successful, which had helped Terry build up his confidence. However, as they had learnt over the past six weeks through radio communications, other patrols had not been so lucky. Inevitably, some had been ambushed *en route* to ambush the Indonesians or CCO. In those attacks, all the SAS men had died. The sergeant leading another group had contracted the jungle disease leptospirosis, which meant that the whole group had to turn back, carrying him all the way while he suffered from a 105-degree temperature and other, more agonizing symptoms. Even more bizarrely, an Australian SAS trooper was gored by an elephant and had to be left in the jungle, on the Indonesian side of the border, while the rest of his group made a two-day trek back across the border to obtain help from a Gurkha camp. Unfortunately, the wounded

THE HEADHUNTERS OF BORNEO

Aussie had died by the time he was found by a casualty-evacuation helicopter pilot determined not to let the man be found by the enemy, dead or alive. As for the others who had died, all identifying items had been removed from their bodies, after which there was a quick burial in an unmarked grave. It was a brutal business.

As Pete started scattering leaves and twigs over the buried Claymores, Terry glanced in both directions, seeing Dead-eye and Alf on one side of him and the newcomer, Ken Burgess, on the other, all of them braced on one knee, the other foot braced on the ground, their Armalites already aimed in different directions at the jungle track. With their faces striped with 'cam' cream and their weapons and clothes also camouflaged, they merged almost perfectly with the tall foliage in which they were hidden.

Dead-eye looked as impassive as ever, Alf looked reasonably intent, and the newcomer, Ken, was the only one showing any tension. So far, Ken had shown his mettle and made no mistakes, but undoubtedly the jungle had taken its toll on him, making him more nervous than he might otherwise have been and causing the others to keep their eyes on him. Some men, no matter how good they were as soldiers, were destroyed by the jungle. Terry had likewise suffered when first exposed to it, but now he was used to it.

After hiding the last of his Claymores, Pete checked the whole area, making doubly sure that it looked absolutely normal, then backed towards the other men, brushing dust, leaves and twigs over his own tracks as he went. When he had finished, the track looked like it had not been trodden on since the dawn of time.

No one spoke. Dead-eye merely acknowledged the thoroughness of Pete's work by silently giving him the thumbs up. Nodding and grinning, Pete knelt in the flattened grass beside the plunger he would use for the detonation of the mines. As SAS troops on patrol were not allowed to leave their weapons at any time – even when sleeping – Pete's Armalite had been slung over his shoulder all the time he was laying the mines. It was still there when he checked the plunger, then rested one hand on it and glanced along the jungle track, to where it disappeared between the trees.

They had neither seen nor heard the Indonesian foot patrol, which was known to be carrying supplies to a full battalion camped north of the River Koemba, but had learnt about it from another SAS patrol, who had caught a glimpse of it from a distant plateau and tracked its direction and speed of movement for over an hour. From those calculations, communicated to this patrol by radio, Dead-eye had been able to calculate the Indonesians' estimated time of arrival at this location. Allowing approximately two hours extra for rest stops and, possibly, an early breakfast, he reckoned that they were due to arrive any time within a two-hour period starting thirty minutes from then.

The wait was tortuous because the men could neither speak to one another nor move from their firing positions. In the absolute silence of the windless *ulu*, the sound of even the slightest movement could carry a long way. Therefore the men had to be ready to fire and to remain in that position, frozen like statues, but with their muscles under strain and rapidly becoming painful, until the action could begin. Luckily, they heard the sounds of distant, advancing movement forty minutes later.

With their weapons already cocked, the SAS troopers did not have to make even that sound. They merely pressed the triggers down slightly and took more careful aim.

The few minutes it took for the Indonesian patrol to appear seemed longer than the previous forty minutes, but eventually the first troops rounded the bend in the path, emerging slowly from the trees and tendrils of early-morning mist, wearing jungle-green fatigues, soft peaked caps and jungle boots.

All of them were slim and had delicate, handsome features. As the rest advanced around the bend, about forty in all, it became clear that they were carrying a variety of weapons, mostly of World War Two vintage, such as Lee-Enfield .303-inch bolt-action rifles and the Soviet PPSh-41 7.62mm sub-machine-gun. They also had hand-grenades clipped to their belts and bandoliers criss-crossing their chests in a manner viewed by the SAS men as suicidal.

The SAS group hidden in the trees did not stop breathing, but each man concentrated on breathing slowly and evenly as he applied a little more pressure to the trigger of his Armalite.

The first of the Indonesian troops reached the first buried Claymore.

Pete placed his free hand beside the other on the detonating plunger, and bunched up his shoulders.

The lead soldier stepped on the buried mine, walked over it and kept walking, kicking up the loose leaves, followed by the others, spread foolishly across the track in twos and threes, treading on one mine, then another, now passing the hidden SAS men, until the last man had stepped on the first mine, buried at a forty-five degree angle from where Pete was leaning forward to press on the plunger.

Pete pressed the plunger all the way down.

The explosions were like thunderclaps, four

mighty roars in one, blowing the soil up and outwards in great fan shapes that spewed smoke and fire. The Indonesians were blown apart, picked up and slammed back down, or slashed to ribbons by the hundreds of razor-sharp slugs that flew with the speed of bullets in all directions.

That the SAS men should open fire with their Armalites simultaneously was almost an act of mercy, since many of the Indonesians not instantly killed were staggering about in the swirling smoke, or writhing on the dust-choked ground, with their skin either scorched and blistered or slashed to the bone and, in many cases, stripped right off the rib cage or limbs, exposing bloody intestines and naked bone.

The hail of SAS bullets stitched through these unfortunates, silencing their demented screams, then moved left and right in a broad arc that took in those who had escaped the blasts of the Claymores and were now retreating into the jungle, firing on the move. Still confused by the explosions, some of them raced straight towards the hidden SAS men, only to be bowled over by another sustained fusillade from the Armalites. Dust billowed up around their falling bodies and blended in with the swirling smoke.

Even before the smoke had cleared, the Indonesians now hidden at the far side of the devastated track

– the soil upturned and blackened, filled with dead men, dismembered limbs, pieces of uniform and broken weapons – were opening fire with their small arms, aiming blindly across the road, through the smoke, and hoping to hit the enemy by accident.

'Bug out!' Dead-eye roared.

Since they were carrying no machine-guns or support weapons, the men were able to jump up and beat a retreat immediately. But as they were doing so, the jungle behind them exploded, showering them with foliage and almost bowling them over.

In fact, Terry *was* bowled over and found himself rolling on the ground until stopped by a tree trunk. Shaking his head to clear it, he glanced to the side, back towards the obliterated path, and saw an enemy soldier rising spectrally from one of the holes caused by a Claymore, his uniform in tatters, pus dripping from blinded eyes, his chest slashed from the left shoulder to just below the right hip, with the skin hanging down like a towel dipped in blood, revealing the rich fruit of his intestines. Obviously sightless, in terrible pain and terrified, he advanced a few feet, waving his scorched hands as if in search of something to cling to, then was cut down by a blast from an Armalite held close to Terry's ear.

Startled, Terry looked up just as Dead-eye grabbed his shoulder, hauled him roughly to his feet, and bawled, 'Run!' Terry ran, holding his own Armalite at the ready, following Dead-eye away from the smoke of the mortar shell, deeper into the jungle. They all kept running for some time, away from the sound of gunfire, weaving between liana-covered tree trunks, changing direction many times, and only stopped when they were sure that the Indonesians would not know where they were. Mortar shells continued to explode well behind them, close to where they had hidden to set up the ambush.

They glanced at one another, then Alf whispered: 'Where's Ken?'

They all looked in different directions, but Ken was nowhere in sight. They waited for a whole minute, but neither saw him nor heard him.

'Damn!' Dead-eye whispered. 'I'd better go back and find him. If he's dead, I have to strip him of identification. If he's alive . . .' Dead-eye shrugged.

Alf glanced at his watch. 'Leave it, boss,' he said.

'No,' Dead-eye replied. 'Wait here. Give me ten minutes. If I don't return, move out.'

'Let's all go,' Pete said. 'If he's wounded, we'll have to try to get him out. If he's dead, we can give you protection while you strip him and bury him.'

'Right,' Dead-eye said.

Without another word, he led them back to where they had come from, hoping that the new man, if still mobile, would have had the sense to follow their tracks. These they had not bothered to cover, knowing that the Indonesians, devastated by the attack, would have followed them only a short distance into the *ulu*. In the event, when they got back to where the enemy mortar shell had exploded (by which time the Indonesians had stopped firing), they found only a small pool of blood and a trail of broken foliage that obviously led directly to where the ambush had taken place. The ground beneath the broken foliage showed the marks of boot heels, indicating that the unfortunate trooper had been wounded by the exploding mortar shell, then captured and dragged away by the Indonesians.

Realizing they were possibly surrounded by Indonesian troops, Dead-eye communicated with sign language, indicating that Ken had been captured and that nothing more could be done for him. Clearly upset, he nevertheless turned back, indicating with another hand signal that they should follow him.

Only when they were well away from the Indonesians did they stop for a rest.

'They'll give Ken a hard time,' Pete said.

'Let's hope he was badly wounded,' Dead-eye

replied, 'and won't last too long. He'll suffer less that way.'

Realizing what they were talking about, Terry shivered involuntarily and made a point of checking his Armalite.

'Time's up,' Dead-eye said crisply.

Badly shaken by Ken's fate, they began the long trek back to the RV, speaking little, staying well spaced apart, and never relaxing for a moment. They did not aim directly for the border, which the Indonesians would have expected, but instead headed south to where the Rivers Sentimo and Koemba met. Dead-eye was out on point, the experienced Alf was Tail-end Charlie, and Terry was behind Pete, his job not only to scout the jungle on both sides, but also to protect the vitally important radio operator or, failing that, the actual radio, which was even more important.

In fact, without the A41 many of the men in the small patrols might have gone mad in the jungle. It was the radio that kept them in touch with one another and removed much of the burden of what might otherwise have been an intolerable burden of isolation. Also, through the radio they could pass on to one another details of enemy troop movements which, for some tactical reason or other, they could not interfere with. It formed a common bond that few wanted to lose.

Four hours later, with the sun high in the sky, they found themselves in the jungle swamps near the confluence of the two rivers. Just before making another hellish slog through waist-deep water, with all the horrors it contained, they contacted other patrols on the A41 and learnt from one of them that according to some Dyaks, the captured SAS trooper had been alive when taken, though suffering from minor wounds to one arm. He had been seen in the enemy camp to which the supply patrol had been heading, lying on the ground with his hands behind his back and tied to his ankles, doubtless awaiting questioning. More news was to be relayed as it came in.

Now even more shaken, Dead-eye's patrol kept on the move, wading through the greenish-brown water while assailed by swarms of flies and mosquitoes. By last light they were in a state of familiar exhaustion, but managed to keep going for another couple of hours until they had reached a dry islet. There they had a meal of dry biscuits, tinned sardines and water, though smoking was not permitted and the hexamine stoves could not be lit for a warming brew-up.

The islet was large enough for them all to sleep on, which was an unexpected luxury that allowed them to awaken relatively refreshed. They moved on for another hour, again wading waist- and sometimes chest-deep through the water, then stopped to have a cold breakfast and try contacting the other groups with the A41. When they did so, they learnt that another Dyak had reported seeing an SAS trooper, obviously Ken Burgess, still bound as before, being dragged roughly across the clearing of the enemy camp and into one of the thatched huts raised on stilts. The tribesman said that he had then heard the soldier screaming for a long time, before being dragged back out again and thrown, still bound, off the veranda of the raised hut. It would have been a long drop.

'Poor bastard!' Alf whispered when Terry, in charge of the radio, had recounted this information to all of them.

'Let's get moving,' Dead-eye snapped.

By noon that day they were out of the swamp and hacking their way through more *belukar* while their booted feet slipped in deepening mud. Now knowing that they were well away from any Indonesians or CCO terrorists, they were able to talk more freely and used the opportunity to express their bitterness over Ken's ordeal.

Dead-eye soon put a stop to it.

'What the fuck do you expect?' he asked contemptuously. 'We chopped those Indos to pieces with our Claymores and bullets, then took off before they could retaliate. Can you imagine what the survivors felt like when they found Burgess wounded? What did you *expect* them to do? Give him a medal?'

'That's no reason to . . .'

'Some of those Indos lost their limbs,' Dead-eye said, cutting Terry off in mid-sentence. 'Others had the flesh stripped off their bones. Still others had burns so severe they couldn't possibly live. That isn't just dying, Trooper. It isn't heroics. It's fucking terrible, it's happening to your friends, and the bastards who did it have disappeared. Then you find one of those bastards. He was left behind by the *other* bastards. He's lying there, wounded, at your feet, and you're not inclined to admire him. Also, you want to find out where his friends are, so you go to work on him. What would *you* have done, Trooper?'

Terry had no answer to that, so he just lowered his eyes.

'Right,' Dead-eye snapped. 'Subject closed. Let's move out, men.'

By last light they had reached a suitable hiding place near Poeri, still on the River Koemba, from where they intended heading north, first to Stass, then on to the RV between Bau and Kuching.

Despite Dead-eye's outburst, the rest of the group was slowly burning up with the thought of what was happening to Ken. Subsequently, when they had made camp, eaten and bedded down in their bashas, they had a night made even more restless by anger and bitterness than it was by the usual flies, mosquitoes, spiders, ants, and the jungle's customary nocturnal cacophony. Their mood was in no way improved when, the following morning, they learnt over the radio that according to the most recent Dyak reports, Ken had been tortured so appallingly that he died before his captors could 'break' him.

'Bastards!' Pete whispered.

'Cunts!' Alf exploded.

'What a shitty thing to do,' Terry said, wiping tears from his eyes. 'I mean . . . Jesus! We can't just forget this. We must *do* something.'

'What we do is head back to the RV,' Dead-eye said firmly. 'Now let's pack up and move out.'

Nevertheless, as they made the short hike to Poeri, from where they intended branching north, Dead-eye knew that what had happened would rankle with the men and maybe make them lose focus. He was therefore almost relieved when, just before they reached Poeri, a longboat containing three uniformed Indonesian soldiers came along the river, heading upstream.

Dead-eye plunged into the shelter of the trees by the river bank, followed immediately by the others.

Kneeling there in the firing position, they watched the boat approaching.

'Well?' Pete asked, his finger itchy on the trigger. 'Do we just let them waltz past?'

'They're not waltzing,' Alf retorted. 'They're rowing like fucking Cambridge dons . . . And that boat's filled with weapons.'

'*And* a dead pig,' Terry observed. 'That means food for a lot of men.'

The three of them turned to stare at Dead-eye. He stared back, then shrugged.

'Let's not argue,' he said.

While Dead-eye, Alf and Terry took aim with their Armalites, Pete unclipped an '80' white-phosphorus incendiary grenade from his webbed belt. 'Let's not take any chances,' he said with grim satisfaction. After unpinning the grenade, he stepped forward for a better view, though still protected by the trees, waited until the boat was abreast of his position, then hurled the grenade.

That movement was enough to attract the attention of the Indonesians in the boat. They glanced up just as Pete stepped back into the trees, raised their eyes even higher when they saw the grenade, then, shouting frantically, threw themselves face-down in the boat as the grenade fell towards them. It actually bounced off the stern, exploding with a thunderous clap, creating a great fountain of rushing, roaring water and smoke illuminated by silvery phosphorus. The stern of the boat was thrown high in the air, forcing the prow down into the water and throwing the soldiers forward, one into the other, with the third one – the one nearest the explosion – bursting into flames and catapulting over his tangled friends, into the river.

Even as the remaining two were struggling to right themselves, one reaching for his rifle, the SAS men on the river bank opened fire with their Armalites, peppering the boat from front to rear, making the soldiers spasm epileptically in a dreadful dance of death as fragments of wood exploded upwards and rained back down over them.

In seconds the two soldiers were dead and the hull of the boat was disintegrating and starting to sink as the SAS men continued firing in an orgy of vengeance. A minute later, when they had finally stopped firing, the boat was practically in pieces, taking in water and going down as the water turned crimson with the blood of the dead men.

The dead men drifted with the boat's debris in swirling blood-red currents, then all evidence of the attack – the wooden flotsam, the bodies, the bloody water – was carried away downstream and eventually disappeared.

'Satisfied?' Dead-eye asked his men.

'Yes, boss!' they replied, one by one.

'Right,' Dead-eye said. 'Let's go.'

As the dead men drifted down river, being swept towards their living comrades in some far off, hidden camp, the SAS patrol headed back across the border, beyond which were more hellish swamps, *belukar* and primary jungle. They tried not to think ahead.

8

Further along the border, on the lower slopes of Gunong Rawan, near Tebedu in the 3rd Division, Sergeant Alan Hunt and Corporal Ralph Sanderson, at the head of their patrol, were moving down from a ridge on a jungle track towards an old Indonesian border-terrorist camp that had been discovered the day before and appeared not to have been used for many months. Nevertheless, as both men knew by now, appearances could be deceptive, so they both advanced on the camp with great care, with Sanderson at the front as lead scout and Hunt second in line.

Hunt was an amiable giant of a man from rural Oxfordshire, with thinning red hair, a constantly flushed, blue-veined face (his heavy drinking only showed there; certainly not in a drinker's paunch) and a body which, for all of its weight, was pure muscle and bone. Thirty-four years old, he had been wounded when engaged with the Gloucestershire

Regiment in their epic battle on the River Injon in Korea, damaging his right arm so badly that it became paralysed and required four years to repair. Once recovered, however, he had applied to the SAS, got in with flying colours, and sustained his already admirable reputation with his work during the Malayan Emergency. Now, here he was, big and wind-blown, yet oddly graceful, moving down the densely forested slope with all the stealth of a tribesman, holding his Armalite at the ready and expert in using it. He was a man worth admiring.

Sanderson admired him. Up at the front on point for the sergeant he knew so well, aware that Indonesian troops could be hiding anywhere, ready to spring an ambush, Sanderson was glad to have Hunt backing him up. Ever since the disaster at Long Jawi, when everyone but Sanderson had lost his life, Sanderson had been more aware than ever of how easy it was to die in this war. A product of the Fifeshire coalmines and the Queen's Own Highlanders, he took pride in being a good soldier and respected only those who felt the same way. Being a good soldier was being a worthy man and Sanderson wanted to be just that.

Reaching a curtain of bamboo, he knelt on the ground and listened intently for any unfamiliar sounds. As no breeze could penetrate the dense canopy of the jungle, let alone reach the ground, and since the animals were always careful to conceal their presence from alien presences, such as humans, Sanderson heard nothing other than the occasional cry of a long-armed gibbon or the squawk of a distant hornbill. Apart from that there was nothing but a total, oddly disturbing silence.

Staring carefully between gaps in the bamboo curtain, he saw the Indonesian camp stretched out just below. Built in a clearing between the jungle and a stream that flowed down to the River Sekayan, it consisted of many bamboo-and-thatched lean-tos without roofs, obviously used as bashas; open-air latrines now covered with swarms of flies; and a series of sunken rectangles that had clearly been gun emplacements and defensive slit trenches. The Indonesians had not bothered to fill in any of these when they moved on. Also, as Sanderson saw when he used his binoculars for a closer inspection, they had not bothered to clean up their debris, which included the black ash of camp-fires, hundreds of cigarette butts, the bones from cooked chicken and pigs, and a lot of rusty food tins with labels stating in Malay that they contained rations for the Indonesian Army. A very careless commander, Sanderson realized, had made no attempt to cover his battalion's tracks.

Lowering his binoculars, Sanderson glanced back

up the wooded slope to see Hunt keeping him covered with his 5.56mm Armalite light automatic rifle. Unseen, because carefully hidden in the jungle behind the sergeant, was the rest of the patrol – three SAS troopers and two Border Scouts – armed with 7.62mm SLRs and now experienced at using them, after four weeks of successful 'Tiptoe Boys' raids. During that time they had travelled light, with no bergens; only their belts and personal weapons. This had made the 'shoot-and-scoot' standard operating procedure much easier and the raids more successful.

Before returning his gaze to the Indonesian camp, Sanderson sniffed the air, trying to catch a tell-tale whiff of anything that would give away another human presence: scent, cigarette smoke or even hair-cream. In the windless jungle such aromas could hang around for hours, which is why the SAS men were careful not to smoke or pamper themselves with hair-creams or aftershave when on patrol. Indeed, so still was the air in this jungle that a man could avoid having his throat cut by smelling the sweat of an approaching enemy. That, in fact, had been the case with Sanderson and he had never forgotten it; no more than he had forgotten his narrow escape at Long Jawi. He considered himself a very lucky man and hoped it would stay that way.

Looking to the front again, Sanderson surveyed the open slope between himself and the camp, which had obviously been cleared by the Indonesians to give their sentries a better view. Seeing no movement, he jumped up and ran forward at the crouch, then dropped down behind another screen of bamboo. As he did so, Hunt advanced behind him, taking up the position Sanderson had just left. The rest of the group then advanced as well, until they were spread out around the position formerly held by their sergeant. They had advanced this way for the past hour, which made the going slow and extremely frustrating.

Again Sanderson looked out between the tall bamboo stalks. At first he saw nothing. Then he thought he saw a slight movement 45 degrees to his right. Turning in that direction, he was startled to see an Indonesian soldier five or six yards away, lying down beside a tree, taking aim with what looked like a Lee-Enfield .303 bolt-action rifle.

Before Sanderson could move the Indonesian opened fire, followed almost simultaneously by a fusillade from his hidden fellow soldiers. Something smashed into Sanderson's leg, bowling him over. Falling, he hit the ground hard, then found himself lying behind a small rock to his left with blood spurting up into his face from a dreadful wound in his left thigh.

'Shit!' he whispered from between clenched teeth, hardly able to hear his own voice above the racket of the battle suddenly raging in front and behind him.

Where the hell was his rifle? Unable to sit upright, he twisted to the side and saw his Armalite just as another Indonesian, who had been lying concealed in the tall grass beyond the rock, also sat up, aiming his Lee-Enfield. The man was so close that Sanderson even saw the tiger's-head emblem on the shoulder of his jungle-green uniform and the panic in his youthful brown eyes.

With no time to spare, Sanderson grabbed his Armalite, blinked blood from his eyes, and fired a short burst that punched the soldier backwards and threw him into the tall grass. He fired another burst to be sure, then wiped more blood from his face and glanced back up the slope.

Hunt was running to his rescue, zigzagging at the crouch between the clumps of bamboo as purple tracers from enemy machine-guns arced past him on both sides. Halfway down, he jerked wildly, dropped his weapon and collapsed, even as Sanderson saw the cloth of his trousers exploding and spitting twin streams of thick blood.

The sergeant fell face-down, but rolled onto his back. He tried to sit up but failed, his shattered legs useless. So, ignoring the bullets stitching the ground on both sides, he rolled back onto his belly, aimed his Armalite and opened fire again, determined to give Sanderson cover.

Behind him, but further up the hill, the rest of the patrol were trying to keep the Indonesians pinned down with a sustained fusillade.

Unable to walk, but still with one good leg, Sanderson managed to stand upright and hop awkwardly up the hill towards Hunt, who was too busy firing to notice his ungainly progress. Once parallel with his friend, but about five yards away, Sanderson dropped to his belly again, gritting his teeth against the pain, and joined the fire-fight.

The Indonesians were spread out on the ground in an arc covering the approach to the empty camp. Lying belly-down, half hidden by the tall grass and clumps of bamboo, they were keeping up a relentless barrage of fire.

Hunt stopped, glanced back over his shoulder, up the hill, and bawled, 'Bug out!' He then turned back and continued firing, enabling the rest of the patrol to make their escape and return to the RV, where they could get help.

As the patrol stopped firing and disappeared over the crest of the hill, one of the Indonesian soldiers, not noticing the wounded men, jumped to his feet and started racing up the hill, heading straight for Hunt. The big, cool-headed sergeant, his hips and legs drenched in blood, fired a short burst from his Armalite and felled the running man. When a second Indonesian stood up, Sanderson put a lethal burst into him, too. The rest of the Indonesians remained on the ground, but kept firing up the hill.

Letting them get on with it, Sanderson rolled onto his back, managed to sit upright, protected by the rock, and examined his wounded leg. It was a mess. In fact, he could not feel it, nor see the wound for the blood still pumping out of it, and so was not sure if the leg was still fixed to his upper thigh or had been torn off by bullets. Delicately wiping away the blood with his fingers, he saw that the bullet, or bullets, had severed the large femoral artery and shattered the femur, though the leg was still joined to the thigh.

Realizing that if he did not stop the bleeding immediately, he would be dead in no time – the blood was pumping out in sprays about fifteen inches long – he hurriedly removed the sweat rag from his forehead, tied a knot in the middle of it, pressed the knot firmly against the artery in the groin, tied the rest of the sweat rag around the limb, wrapped the ends of the rag around the handle of his commando knife and then twisted the knife until the cloth had tightened painfully, with the knot pressed like a vice on the artery, cutting off the supply of blood. When the blood had stopped pumping, he tied another knot in the cloth, completing the makeshift tourniquet, then injected himself with a shot of morphine and heaved a sigh of relief.

Looking up, he saw that the Indonesians were still firing at him and Hunt. Though the bullets were turning the ground into a convulsion of boiling dust and spinning foliage, Sanderson crawled over to his friend, who, when he saw him coming, rolled onto his back and gazed up at the sky.

'I can't move my damned legs,' he said.

Hunt's face was a white mask glistening with sweat. He had been shot in the hip, though his wound was much worse than Sanderson's. The bullet had entered the left hip, almost severing the sciatic nerve, thereby paralysing and rendering numb that leg. While the hole punched in the front of the thigh had been only slightly larger than the .303-inch bullet that caused it, it had enlarged as the bullet passed through the pelvic opening, destroying a fist-sized mass of muscle in the right buttock and therefore paralysing that leg as well. Besides losing a mass of blood, Hunt had lost the use of both legs.

'Fucking mess, eh?' he said, gritting his teeth.

''Fraid so, boss,' Sanderson replied.

Another sustained burst of fire came from the

Indonesian positions and more green tracer shot upwards and whipped past them, just a few feet away.

'Russian RPD machine-gun,' Hunt said. 'I know. I saw the whites of his fucking eyes. Then he copped me.' He winced and looked down at the blood soaking his trousers around the tattered hole. 'Christ!' he said softly. 'At least it's not a tourniquet job.' He had not noticed the crude tourniquet on Sanderson's leg. 'I think I can fix this.'

While Sanderson kept the Indonesians pinned down with single shots from his Armalite, thus conserving ammunition while remaining a viable threat, Hunt removed two shell dressings from his first aid kit, worked them in and under the torn cloth around the bloody wound, gritted his teeth and pressed them into the hole, then held them in position by wrapping his sweat rag around the thigh. After completing the job with a shot of morphine, he rolled onto his belly, beside Sanderson, and picked up his Armalite to fire on the Indonesians.

'Shoot-and-scoot,' he said.

'What does that mean?' Sanderson asked him.

'It means we have to prevent casualties when there's no point in fighting to hold ground. It means that in a situation like this, you pocket your pride and piss off. It means that we all scoot independently for the RV and that if a man is incapacitated, you have to leave him, at least temporarily, to prevent further casualties.'

'Piss on that,' Sanderson said.

'No,' Hunt replied. 'We don't piss on that. You go back to the RV and join up with the others. If you find enough men for reinforcements, you can come back to find me. If you still find the Indos here, you piss off and leave me to my fate. If, on the other hand, the Indos have gone you can pick me up for the CasEvac and early pension.'

'I don't like it,' said Sanderson gloomily.

'It's not a request. Get going, Corporal.'

Sanderson squeezed the sergeant on the shoulder, then, reluctantly, started crawling up the hill, dragging his wounded leg. As he did so, Hunt opened fire with his Armalite, still on automatic, laying down a sustained burst that would ensure the enemy kept their heads down for a short while. Sanderson used that brief lull in their fire to get up the hill as quickly as possible, though his numbed leg did not make it easy for him. He did, however, manage to clear the breast of the hill just as Hunt stopped firing to reload and the Indonesians let rip again.

Glancing back over his shoulder, Sanderson saw the ground around Hunt turned into a nightmarish convulsion of spitting dust and exploding foliage. Then Sanderson crawled away, down the other side. The sudden silence from the other side of the hill convinced him that Hunt had been killed in that final fusillade. Shocked, but determined to survive, Sanderson crawled on.

It was not an easy journey. Unable to stand, he had to crawl most of the way, stopping at intervals to loosen the tourniquet and let the blood flow a little, thus diminishing the chances of gangrene. Then he tightened it and moved on again.

Just as he had to keep stopping to loosen and tighten the tourniquet, so he had to stop to give himself repeated injections of morphine, which eased the excruciating pain when the crawling made the pieces of the shattered femur grind together. He could even hear them grinding, which made the pain seem worse, and he also knew that the sharp-edged, broken bones could, when grinding together, sever more arteries and kill him that way.

Nevertheless, he kept crawling back towards the RV, through mud, over felled logs, between tangled clumps of thorny bushes, stopping only to attend to the wound, then starting forward again.

By nightfall, he had managed to crawl only 500 yards, though each yard had seemed like a mile. Finding a pig hole beneath a fallen tree, he crawled into it, deep into the pools of mud, and took another shot of morphine before falling asleep.

Sergeant Hunt had not been killed by the Indonesians. In fact, after that final fusillade, they gave up, assuming the enemy was gone, and retreated back across the empty camp, then into the jungle. They did not reappear.

Seeing that they were gone, Hunt pulled himself into the cover of a clump of bamboo, injected himself with more morphine to combat the pain, checked that the bandages in his enormous wound were still stemming the blood, then passed out.

He was unconscious most of the night. Just before first light, after breakfasting on chocolate from his escape belt, he injected himself yet again, then began to crawl up the hill, determined to follow Sanderson to the RV. So bad was his leg that he could only do this by using his elbows: digging them into the soft earth and pulling himself forward, inch by inch. This he did until, by late afternoon, he had managed to drag himself to the top of the ridge, which was only 400 yards from the scene of the fire-fight. Exhausted, he lay there face-down for a couple of hours, then rolled over and studied the afternoon sky. Seeing no friendly choppers up there, he rolled back onto his stomach and recommenced his dreadful journey.

This time he was forced to elbow his way through a stretch of *belukar*, which was filled with thorny undergrowth that cut him all over, depriving him of more blood. As secondary jungle is the haunt of wild pigs, Hunt soon found himself crawling through a maze of runs where the pigs had rooted in the soil for food. These runs were filled with mud containing many leeches, which were attracted by the smell of his thorn wounds and attached themselves to him to drink the blood. Too weak to fend them off, Hunt soon found himself covered in mounds of writhing leeches and knew that he was losing more blood than he could reasonably afford, given what he was also losing from the gruesome bullet wound.

Still he crawled on until, like Sanderson, he found a pig hole into which he could crawl for the night. There, while he tried to sleep, swarms of fat, shiny bluebottles clustered on his wound and laid eggs that turned into grubs to make the wound fester. If he did not get the wound tended to soon, he would be in serious trouble.

Using his elbows for leverage, though the skin there was rubbed raw and giving him more agony, the next morning he managed to crawl another 1000 yards. What kept him going was the knowledge that the rest of the patrol would have gone to find the infantry – the 1st Battalion of the 6th

Gurkha Rifles – and bring them back to find him, and perhaps Sanderson too.

In fact, he thought that he might come across Sanderson at any moment, which was another incentive to keep going. In the event, neither Sanderson nor the Gurkhas materialized.

That night, now even more exhausted, as well as being in agony, Hunt injected himself with another shot of morphine and fell into the sleep of the dead. He was not dead, however, and next morning awakened to the distinct smell of coffee. Not realizing at first where he was, and imagining that he was awakening in his own basha in the spider at Kuching, he turned his head and saw an Indonesian soldier climbing a nearby durian tree.

Freezing cold where he was lying, suddenly remembering where he was and that he was seriously wounded, he watched as the Indonesian soldier, having gained his desired position, stretched out along the branch of a tree and picked off some of its spiky fruit, the flesh of which was edible. Lowering his gaze, he saw a whole group of enemy soldiers squatting at the base of a nearby tree, around a communal pot of rice or tapioca. Looking up again, he saw the first soldier staring straight at him from the tree.

Hunt froze. He had to force himself to remember

that although he was looking up into the eyes of the man in the tree, that man could not necessarily see him where he was lying in a hollow in the ground, caked as he was with mud and covered with foliage. And yet he could not be sure of that, so his heart started racing.

At that moment a British Army Air Corps Sikorsky S-55 Whirlwind helicopter appeared in the sky, flying in low over the jungle, obviously searching for the two missing SAS men. Seeing it, Hunt was flooded with relief and reached automatically for the SARBE rescue beacon on his webbed belt. As he was doing so, the Indonesian in the tree and his friends on the ground all glanced up at the helicopter. Some of them pointed at it, chattering excitedly, then bent over to pick up their weapons.

Suddenly realizing that the Whirlwind would be in danger if he fired his SARBE beacon and encouraged it lower, Hunt removed his hand from his belt and decided to take his chances.

When the Whirlwind passed overhead without coming within firing range, the Indonesians put down their weapons and returned to their breakfast. Eventually, the soldier in the tree, who clearly had not seen the SAS man, clambered back down to the ground, where he passed out the durian fruit to his friends.

Hunt lay there and watched them, gritting his teeth against the pain of his wounded leg, but not daring to risk the movement required to inject more morphine. Eventually, after what seemed like hours, but was in fact an hour later, the Indonesians completed their breakfast, picked up their weapons and marched away, quickly melting back into the *ulu*.

Sighing with relief, Hunt injected himself with more morphine, cleaned his wound of pus and maggots, finished off the last of his chocolate, then began crawling forward again, using his bloody elbows as leverage. By noon he had managed a few hundred yards more, but was stopped by exhaustion. Falling asleep, or perhaps rendered unconscious by the return of the pain, he woke in the late afternoon, feeling weaker and more disorientated.

Though now convinced that he was fading fast, he had enough strength of mind to inject himself with more morphine and start another exhausting forward crawl. Convinced as he was that he could not survive another night without aid, he was not encouraged by the fact that the jungle here was *belukar*, so dense with tree stumps, felled logs, saplings, thorns and general undergrowth that a helicopter would not have been able to land.

Nevertheless, he kept going and, two hours later,

as the sun was beginning to set and the nocturnal chorus of the insects was building, he came out of the *belukar*, into more accessible terrain. There, however, beyond the darkening mountain, black rain clouds were spreading across the sky, threatening a tropical storm. No helicopter could fly through such weather.

Hunt was silently praying that the storm would not begin when he heard distant thunder. No, it was not that. It was another, more constant sound. He glanced up as the sound grew louder, becoming a rhythmic throbbing, then an actual roaring. Something blotted out the sinking sun and cast its shadow over him as a violent wind tore leaves off the trees and whipped the leaves off the ground. It was the same chopper, coming back to find him.

Knowing that the Indonesians were nowhere near this territory, he unclipped the SARBE beacon from his belt and sent up a rescue signal. Hearing the SARBE's bleep, the pilot descended vertically, wobbling from side to side, but could find no space clear enough for a landing.

Like a blood-splattered crab, Hunt crawled out on bent elbows to where he could be seen, then raised his right hand to wave frantically.

The pilot dropped until he was almost touching the trees, with the rotor blades actually chopping leaves off. While the chopper hovered there, in danger of crashing, a crewman threw the rescue strop out on its lengthy cables. It plunged to just above the ground, jerked back up, then bobbed in mid-air, just above the wounded man.

Still unable to move his legs, Hunt had an agonizing time with the strop, which kept swinging to and fro just above his outstretched fingers; but eventually he managed to grab it and twist himself around until he could fit it under his armpits. Still holding his Armalite in one hand, he signalled with the other for the crewman to winch him up. The helicopter ascended as he was being winched up and soon he found himself swinging in the sky above the vast, darkening jungle.

Up there he was as free as a bird.

As Sergeant Hunt was being flown to the Gurkhas' jungle post at Sain, from where he would be casualty-evacuated to Kuching Hospital, 45 miles away, Corporal Sanderson was sleeping in another pig hole not far from where his friend had been rescued.

Dangerously weak from loss of blood, pain and the exhaustion of having to crawl for miles on his belly, Sanderson had a very troubled sleep and woke at dawn feeling dreadful. Nevertheless, he kept going. He was only 5000 yards from the Gurkha camp at Sain, but it might as well have been that number of miles. After another 200 yards, he was in a state of almost total exhaustion, bordering on hallucination, and felt even more unreal when he came across the bergens that the team had left behind to make the 'shoot-and-scoot' operation easier. By now the bergens were rotted by damp and fungus, with what little food remained after the ransacking of pigs and honey-bears as rotted as the rucksacks themselves.

Sanderson did, however, find a water bottle filled with drinkable water and used this to quench his raging thirst. Then, forgetting in his rising delirium that the most likely place the choppers would look for him would be where the bergens had been left, he crawled on, determined to find the RV.

By last light he had covered 1000 yards, a mere fifth of the distance he had to go. Not knowing where he was, and increasingly delirious, he did not even bother trying to find a pig hole for the night, but just crawled to a moss-covered tree and propped himself upright, surrounded by thick liana, under a great umbrella of razor-sharp palm leaves. There he finished off the last of his chocolate, washed it down with the last of his water, then closed his eyes and tried to sleep, reconciling himself to death and crazily amused at the thought of his corpse being eaten by wild pigs or other jungle animals.

Better than compo food, he thought as the darkness descended. I can take pride from that.

Either dreaming or hallucinating, he was jerked back to reality by a faint thrashing sound not far away. Opening his eyes, he saw only the gloomy *ulu*, but then he heard the thrashing sound again. It was not very loud – it was almost stealthy – but it was coming towards him.

Instinctively trying to move, Sanderson was whiplashed by the pain in his wounded leg and had to stop himself from crying aloud. Nevertheless, the sudden, stabbing pain, accompanied by a spurt of leaking blood where he had loosened the tourniquet, had the virtue of making him more alert. Still sitting upright against the trunk of the tree, he pulled the Armalite off his shoulder, rested it on his knees, then held it up with the stock pressed against his right hip.

Glancing down, he saw that his sudden movement had loosened the tourniquet more and now blood was pumping out at a dangerous rate. Glancing to where the thrashing sound was growing louder, he saw branches being parted in a way that suggested he was not faced with an advancing animal, but an army patrol.

Sanderson set the Armalite to automatic, then cocked the weapon.

The foliage just ahead parted and the first of

the soldiers emerged – small, brown-faced men, carrying Armalites and SLRs, all with familiar yellow flashes on their soft jungle caps. It was the Gurkhas from Sain.

Sanderson smiled and lowered his Armalite, letting it rest in the grass beside him, though still under his hand. His other hand was covered in his own blood, but he raised it in welcome.

'Hi, there!' he said.

He passed out when they picked him up, placed him on a stretcher and carried him the remaining 4000 yards back to the base camp at Sain.

9

'You have to return to the River Koemba north-west of Poeri,' Major Callaghan insisted, sitting behind his desk in his office in the Haunted House in Kuching, smoking a cigarette, blowing smoke rings and watching them disappear. 'It's there that the Indonesians are believed to have one of their main staging posts for men and supplies going eastward to Seluas, a good-sized trading settlement where the Indonesian Division has its base. That longboat you shot up on your way back was probably heading for there.'

'Why us?' Dead-eye asked, unwrapping some chewing gum and popping it into his mouth.

'What's the matter, Sergeant Parker? Don't you *want* this lovely job?'

'I'll do any job you give me,' Dead-eye replied. 'I just wondered if we were picked for a specific reason when we've just got back from there.'

'Not quite the same area, but close enough.'

151

Callaghan pursed his lips and blew another smoke ring. Even in the afternoon, with the sun blazing outside, he had the shutters down to keep the sunlight out. It made the office pretty dark, Dead-eye thought. Like a haunted house, in fact. 'Six other patrols attempted to reach specific points on the river near Poeri, but failed because the river marshes were too deep. You lot actually made it. So I'd like you to go back there, but this time to find that staging post at Seluas and put a stop to it. You can choose your own spot for setting up a river watch and causing a little mayhem near the town. I'm sure you'll enjoy it.'

Dead-eye grinned slightly, then glanced at the maps spread out on Callaghan's desk. 'Can I see those?'

'Of course!' Callaghan dropped his feet off the desk and turned the maps around to enable Dead-eye to study them. This Dead-eye could do because he had been briefed at West Brigade's HQ, where, as a trained reader of aerial photographs, he had been able to spot the spur that had enabled the recent patrols to recce the unexplored territory known as the Gap. Now, studying the aerial pictures laid out before him, he was soon able to find another spur of the low border hills. It pointed towards a broad bend in the river.

'There,' he said, putting his finger on the spot as

Callaghan stood up and walked around the desk to peer over his shoulder. 'This finger of dry ground here. It appears to peter out three quarters of a mile short of the river, but it might actually reach it. Usually, when it's this close on the map, there's a dry strip somewhere. I'll opt for that route.'

'I'm sure you're right,' Callaghan said. 'You usually are.' He went back around his desk and sat down again. 'So who do you plan to take? Sergeant Hunt and Corporal Sanderson are obviously out of the picture – both back in Blighty, badly hurt, up for commendations and/or medals – so you'll have to be the man in charge and pick your own team.'

'That's nice,' Dead-eye said. He was not too concerned about the loss of Sanderson and Hunt, since both of them actually came from A Squadron and he had never got to know them all that well. He had, however, respected them and visited them at the Kuching Hospital when he was there for a couple of days of so-called recuperation leave. While in reasonably good spirits, both men had been in a bad way physically, with Sanderson likely to lose a good inch or so off his wounded leg and neither man likely to continue to serve with the SAS in their original capacity. More likely they would be given some kind of desk job in the 'Kremlin' in Hereford, which was not the kind of thing that would satisfy them. Still, they had been stoical about it and Dead-eye admired them both.

'I want the same men,' he told Callaghan. 'Welsh as demolition expert and number two; Laughton as medical specialist and photographer; young Malkin as signaller and for general back-up.'

'I'm not sure I want someone so inexperienced for this job.'

'He's not inexperienced any more. He's been through a lot.'

'No problems?'

'None.'

'I thought at first he was showing signs of instability – particularly regarding the *ulu*.'

'He was, but he got over it and has certainly proved himself since then. Not just once – a lot more than that – so he's shown some consistency. He's earned his winged dagger, boss.'

Callaghan smiled. 'Anything you say, Dead-eye. If you want him, you've got him.' He stubbed his cigarette out, clasped his hands behind his head, placed his feet back on the desk and gazed reflectively at the large wooden-bladed fan turning above them. 'God!' he exclaimed softly. 'Remember Welsh and Laughton in Malaya? A right pair of wide boys, troublemakers, always right on the edge there. Neither I nor Sergeant Lorrimer – God rest his soul – thought they'd last another year with the regiment. In fact, both of us were preparing to RTU them, but that didn't happen.'

'The Telok Anson swamp,' Dead-eye said, recalling its singular horrors and how it had matured Welsh and Laughton, instead of destroying them. All bad things had their good side.

Callaghan sighed. 'God, yes. What a hole! And those two came good in the end, which just goes to show.' He continued to study the fan for a while, then lowered his gaze again, grinning at Dead-eye. 'Still miss Lorrimer?'

'Yes.'

'He *was* a good man.' Callaghan glanced down at the maps spread out on his desk, then ran his forefinger lightly, with barely concealed yearning, along the dotted line that indicated the River Koemba. 'I wish I was going with you,' he said. 'I'm not keen on desk jobs.'

'You're good at it, boss.'

Callaghan nodded, but his face revealed his feeling of loss. 'Yes, I'm good at it. I'm a wizard at intelligence. I'm even better at planning and strategy, which makes me invaluable . . . But I'd rather be out there in the field, doing what I was born to do.'

'Maybe you'll get back to it.'

'We both know that's not true. This will be my last tour with the regiment, then it's back to 3 Commando and another promotion.'

'What's wrong with promotion?'

'It leads to even more <u>adm</u>inistration and a lot of rather boring socializing in the name of public relations. I'll be a stuffed dummy for the Army, attending functions, shaking hands, signing the odd document – in fact, doing all the things I detest. That's what's wrong with promotion.'

'Refuse.'

'I can't. It's my age. It comes to us all.'

'Me as well, boss.'

'But you're luckier, Dead-eye. *You're* an NCO. That means you can stay with the SAS for as long as you like – at least until your retirement. Even when it gets to the stage where you can't fight, you can stay with the Training Wing in Hereford, doing good work.'

'To me, doing good work in the Training Wing is the same as you shaking hands. It's just not my style.'

Callaghan grinned in that same sad way. 'No, I suppose not. I just can't imagine it.' As if troubled by his own words, he glanced down at the maps, then looked up again and changed the subject, trying to sound lighter. 'So Laughton's your photographer.'

'Yes,' Dead-eye said.

'Can he actually handle a camera?'

'Yes.'

'Make sure he takes a lot of pictures.'

'I will, boss. Don't worry. So when do we leave?'

'First light.'

'Tomorrow?'

'You've had your leave, Dead-eye. You *hate* leave. So it's first light tomorrow.'

'Right, boss, that's fine. I'd better go and brief the men.'

'Yes, Dead-eye, you do that.'

Dead-eye left Callaghan's office and stepped onto the veranda outside, where he had to shade his eyes against the morning's fierce light. Adjusting to the glare, he saw the trees of the jungle rising in a rich green tangle above the loose scattering of longhouses and warehouses along the dusty road leading into the town. While most of the regular Army, Marine Commandos and Gurkhas in the area were living in converted warehouses and even less comfortable accommodation, Callaghan had cleverly outflanked the billeting arrangements by murmuring about lack of space for his men, the possible requirement for unnecessarily expensive hotels, and so forth, with the result that his men now had their bashas in a large and comfortable Chinese merchant's house.

Entering the building, which was not far from the Haunted House, Dead-eye made his way to the rear, where the men had turned the largest room into their spider. He found Pete Welsh, Alf Laughton and Terry Malkin in there, the first two sitting together on one bed, smoking, drinking beer and playing cards, the latter listening to the BBC World News Service while reading James Joyce's *Ulysses*.

'How can you do both?' Dead-eye asked him.

Terry swung his legs off the edge of the bed and sat up, almost at attention. Although he had proved himself as a soldier, he was still in awe of Dead-eye.

'Don't know, boss. Just can.'

'You understand that *Ulysses*, do you? I heard it was difficult.'

'I don't really understand it all, but I like the bits I *do* understand.'

'That sounds logical, Trooper. We're going back on patrol tomorrow morning, so come and hear what it's all about.'

Dead-eye walked over to where Pete and Alf were playing cards in a haze of cigarette smoke, only breaking their concentration long enough to swig some more beer. However, they did look up when Dead-eye stopped beside the bed with Terry beside him.

'Oh, oh,' Pete said. 'It's Sergeant Parker.'

'This can only mean trouble,' Alf added.

'It's work,' Dead-eye told them, then filled them in at length on the situation, ignoring the other men in the long room, most of whom were listening to the radio, playing cards, reading or writing letters home. When he was finished, he asked, 'Any questions?'

'Yes,' Alf said. 'How come we only got a week-end off after all that shit?'

'We didn't want to spoil you,' Dead-eye said.

'Spoil me?' Alf replied. 'I hardly had time to dip my wick before I had to pull it out again and hurry back to the base. Two days, meaning one night, in that town doesn't do you much good, boss.'

'I'm amazed you could get it in,' Dead-eye said. 'I think that calls for a Mention in Dispatches. Remind me to remind Major Callaghan when he's nothing better to do.'

'*Terry* got it in,' Pete said, grinning slyly at Alf as the butt of their humour blushed deep crimson. 'At least we saw him leave the bar with a whore who had her hand on his arse.'

Terry blushed even more. 'Come on, fellas, knock it off! I didn't tell them anything, Sarge. What I do is my business.'

'Was this a whorehouse?' Dead-eye asked.

'You might call it that,' Alf said. 'It was a bar with a couple of rooms at the back and bedsprings that made too much noise. That's how we know

159

Terry dipped *his* wick: we could hear all the squeaking.'

'From him,' Pete said.

'That's a lie!' Terry burst out.

'I hope you used a rubber,' Dead-eye said. 'The whores here are diseased.'

'She wasn't a whore!' Terry protested.

'She was *nice*,' Pete said. 'She was so nice she let us share her around when Terry walked out the door.'

'That's not true!' Terry exploded again.

'He's in love,' Alf explained.

'He'll get her out of his system,' Dead-eye said, 'when we're back on the border.'

'When?' Pete asked.

'Tomorrow.'

'What time?'

'Don't tell me,' Alf said wearily, blowing smoke. 'We move out at first light.'

'What a bright boy you are,' Dead-eye told him. 'First light it is. In fact, I'm letting you sleep till then, just to prove I'm a nice guy. You can get out of your bashas at first light and have a quick shower and shave. Breakfast at six-thirty sharp, then a line-up at the quartermaster's stores at seven, on the dot. You'll have one hour to get kitted out, collect your weapons and get to the chopper. We lift off at eight. Any questions?'

'Yes,' Pete said. 'Is Terry in love with his whore? Has he picked up gonorrhoea or syphilis? What do you think, Sarge?'

'I think your two-day leave was two days too many and that bastards like you are safer up on the border, fighting the Indos. Tomorrow you'll all be back where you belong and I think you should thank me.'

'Thank you, Sarge,' Pete said.

'I kiss your feet,' Alf added.

'I think you're *all* bloody disgusting,' Terry said, then returned to his bed.

'He'll make a good trooper,' Dead-eye told the other two, then he grinned, turned away and walked out of the barracks, back into the scorching sun of noon. He could hardly wait to get out of there.

10

Dead-eye's patrol checked their weapons and drew ammunition. This was limited to the amount they could comfortably carry when engaged in 'shoot-and-scoot' operations. Each man therefore packed in his bergen only the clothes he considered vitally essential for this patrol, as well as his basic rations: oatmeal blocks, sardines, Oxo cubes, small tins of cheese, biscuits, a little sugar, tea or coffee, milk in a tube, and twenty-four blocks of dehydrated meat – in all weighing less than 1lb for each day's meals. Permitted by Dead-eye were the little extras personally preferred by each man to add taste to the basic rations, such as curry powder, cigarettes or sweets. All of them carried a piece of strong nylon cord, which could be used for many things, including rigging up hammocks in the swamps and making tourniquets. They also carried a parachute-silk sleeping bag with a poncho to keep out the worst of the tropical rainstorms.

Since streams are obvious camp-sites, always under surveillance, invariably a patrol makes its hides a good distance from water. For this reason, each man was given a large water bottle which he could fill up in a stream and then carry to the hide, where he would purify the water with tablets before drinking it or otherwise using it.

As photographer, Alf naturally had high-power binoculars and a camera, a robust 35mm SLR, with which he would take shots of men, boats, vehicles, military camps, longhouses and even areas likely to be of interest to the staff of military intelligence, who could study the photos later at their leisure.

'If I get enough practice,' he informed Pete, 'I'll be a pin-up photographer when we get home – all bare arse and tits.

'I'm a knickers and bra man myself,' Pete confessed as he manoeuvred some more kit into his packed bergen. 'It's my little perversion.'

'I'll be catering for all kinds,' Alf assured him, 'so you've no need to worry there. I'll even photograph some whores for young Terry here to fall in love with.'

'You pair are sick!' Terry snapped.

In fact, it was Terry who had the heaviest load, because, besides the A41 radio set and spare battery, its aerials and the code-books, he also carried on his belt the SARBE radio beacon. To compensate

163

for this, his rations were divided among the others, purely for the purpose of transportation.

'The things we have to do for these newcomers,' Pete complained melodramatically, trying to find some spare space in his already packed bergen for his share of Terry's rations.

'I didn't ask you to,' Terry said. 'It was Dead-eye. He said . . .'

'Sucking up to Sarge goes a long way,' Alf interjected, holding a bar of Terry's chocolate in front of his groin and pantomiming the act of masturbation over it. 'If you're willing to get down on your hands and knees, sweet things will come your way.'

'I want my rations back,' Terry said, outraged by the others' attempts to humiliate him.

'You're not getting them,' Dead-eye said. 'I've weighed everyone's kit and you're overweight, so these lads have to share the weight.'

'Then tell them to shut up.'

'My lips are sealed,' Pete said. 'I try to be nice and I'm rejected and struck dumb by grief.'

'If you don't seal those lips,' Dead-eye said, 'I'll do the job for you. So seal them and shut up.'

'Yes, boss!' Pete said briskly.

For this particular mission, each man was given a 7.62mm SLR instead of the 5.56mm Armalite assault rifle. This caused a lot of 'honking', or complaining.

'Bloody useless,' Alf grumbled.

'A fucking toy,' was Pete's verdict.

'You're wrong,' Dead-eye insisted. 'Its hitting power is more likely to damage river craft than higher-velocity bullets from an Armalite. That's why we're switching.'

'I still prefer the Armalite,' Pete said. 'It's smaller and lighter and fully automatic. The SLR is only semi-automatic and an awful lot heavier.'

'I agree,' Alf said.

'That doesn't change the fact,' Dead-eye informed them, 'that the SLR has a more powerful cartridge and bullet, which makes it better for long-range firing and penetration. It'll therefore be a lot more effective when attacking the river boats.'

'Not so effective in a fire-fight,' Pete persisted.

'We shoot and scoot, Pete,' Alf said.

'I hate that,' Pete objected. 'I like to stand and fight.'

'We're not concerned with body counts,' Dead-eye told him. 'We want to stop their supplies. So stop whinging and get on with your packing. We haven't got all day.'

Once equipped, they applied the usual camou-flage to themselves and their weapons, checked each other's camouflage and kit – ensuring in the latter case that nothing was loose – then strapped their bergens on their backs, picked up their weapons, and left the spider.

Once outside the Chinese merchant's house, in the early-morning mist, they were driven in a Bedford RL 4x4 three-tonner along a road lined with *belukar* and soaring trees to Kuching airfield, where they boarded an RAF Twin Pioneer for the short flight to Lundu.

'I seem to have spent half my life in fucking aeroplanes,' Alf complained as he strapped himself into his seat.

'Better than public transport,' Pete replied. 'And certainly better than walking.'

'This is the part I hate most,' Terry chipped in. 'I hate being cooped up.'

'Except in cramped rooms on squeaking beds with delectable little Indonesian whores.'

'Oh, shut up, Pete!' Terry said, flaring up again. 'You've got a mind like a sewer.'

'And a nose for the dirt.' Dead-eye was looking grimly at Pete. 'Why not can it, Trooper?'

'My silence is now guaranteed, boss. Whoops! There she blows!'

The engines of the Pioneer had just roared into life. Less than a minute later she was taxiing along the runway, preparing to take off. Within minutes she was in the air, flying over another spectacular panorama of jungle, mountains, winding rivers and aerial bridges spanning deep, narrow gorges with torrents raging through them. A fine curtain of silver-grey mist covered the green splendour of the *ulu* and made it seem dreamlike, reminding all of them, except Terry, of their days in Malaya. They were memories of heroism and horror, of friendship and grief. The men were silent throughout the flight.

The journey was short, twenty minutes, and soon they were disembarking at Lundu, where another Bedford was waiting to transfer them to a familiar Wessex Mark 1 helicopter, piloted by their old friend, Lieutenant Ralph Ellis of the Army Air Corps. Ellis was biting into an apple and grinning sardonically.

'This is getting to be a bad habit,' he told them. 'Dragging me out of bed at this ungodly hour. This,' he added, waving the apple, 'is the only breakfast I've had.'

'We haven't *had* breakfast yet,' Pete reminded him. 'You fly-boys have got an easy life – even apples for breakfast!'

'He's a healthy lad,' Alf said.

'With a little paunch,' Pete pointed out.

'And a little bald spot on his head, getting bigger each day.'

'It's the shock of being dragged out of bed this

early,' Alf explained to his friend. 'He's not used to the hard life.'

'And you jokers,' Ellis said, wrapping the apple core in a piece of paper and putting it into his tunic pocket, 'have forgotten how to show respect for an officer. So shut up and get in.'

'Yes, dear!' Alf and Pete sang, clambering into the chopper, with Dead-eye and Terry right behind them.

The lift to the LZ took less than thirty minutes, and took them over the sheer green canopy of the jungle in brightening sunlight. Ellis dropped them near the frontier with Kalimantan, due north of Achan. Unable to land, he descended between the trees, dangerously close to their branches, and hovered there, creating a storm, just above the jungle floor.

The men jumped out one by one, burdened with weapons and bergens, and melted into the *ulu* before the Wessex had even started climbing. Already hidden by the soaring trees, the men grouped together near the LZ, whiplashed by the slipstream of the rotors but waiting until the helicopter had ascended and was heading away from them. Only when it had disappeared beyond the jungle canopy, into the silvery-blue, cloud-smudged sky, did they prepare to move off.

'I think it's highly fucking unlikely,' Alf said,

'that the Indos and CCO won't have seen that chopper drop us off.'

'I've no doubt that they saw us,' Dead-eye replied calmly, 'but since we're still on our own side of the border, they'll assume we're just another bunch of reinforcements moving up to join the border battalions. They won't suspect for a moment that we're planning to cross into Kalimantan.'

'Still, the quicker we get out of here the better,' Pete said.

'I agree,' Dead-eye replied quickly, 'so let's hit the road, lads.'

They marched away from the clearing, heading into the *ulu*, on the first leg of the route that Dead-eye had mapped out.

It would not be an easy route.

11

They headed roughly due south, following Dead-eye's compass bearings, intending to turn due west seven days later, which would lead them to the finger spur seen on the maps. The first day's march was uneventful and relatively easy, through primary jungle that did not require hacking, even though it was as humid as always and oppressively dark. During this first day's hike they stopped frequently to rest and listen for enemy movements, broke for a lunch of water and dried biscuits, but otherwise kept going until nightfall, trying to get as far as they could while they felt reasonably fresh.

After selecting a suitable LUP, they had supper, which was another cold and unedifying meal. Then, while Pete and Alf sat out on point, keeping their eyes and ears open for enemy movements, Dead-eye gave Terry the first of his daily reports, to be transmitted, encoded, to Major Callaghan back at HQ.

They moved on at first light the following morning. Dead-eye was out in front on point as the scout, followed by Pete as his number two, then Terry with the radio, and Alf as Tail-end Charlie. Each man was concentrating intently on his individual defensive arc, holding his SLR at the ready and prepared to use it.

This constant watchfulness was more stressful than expected, though their arduous SAS training had prepared them for it. Though less burdened with kit than the others, Dead-eye had the most demanding job, being far ahead of the main group and therefore dangerously isolated. He needed to be constantly vigilant, and could not relax for a second as he watched and listened for likely ambush positions or signs of enemy movements up ahead. As he also had to check the jungle floor and the lower branches of the trees for mines or booby-traps, he was always under great stress, though he handled this better than most, in his deadly calm, cold-blooded way.

Pete had a dual role. His first function was to give the point man cover should the enemy attack. The second was to glance back over his shoulder every few minutes to ensure that the signaller, carrying the all-important radio, was still in sight and unharmed. In conducting this visual check, he constantly alternated from left to right, and so also managed to scan the *ulu* on both sides of the track. This ceaseless vigilance – to the front, to both sides, and to the rear – was also more demanding, both physically and mentally, than it would have appeared to an inexperienced onlooker.

Terry's primary function was to transmit messages, check constantly whether there were any incoming ones, and to protect the radio with his life. But he, too, had to keep his eyes on the men ahead, on the *ulu* on both sides of the track, and on the Tail-end Charlie, a good distance behind him, to ensure that he had not been picked off quietly by a silenced rifle, a knife, a garrotte, or even a booby-trap.

Bringing up the rear, Alf's primary duty was to check every few minutes that no Indonesians were stalking the patrol. This he did by turning his back on the patrol and walking backwards at regular intervals, scanning the *ulu* on both sides as well as directly behind him. As it is with the scout on point, so the most stressful part of the Tail-end Charlie's job is being relatively isolated from the main group, always wondering if someone is sneaking up from the rear to dispatch you with a bullet in the spine or slit your throat with a dagger. The Tail-end Charlie also has to keep a keen eye on the signaller directly ahead of him, and ensure that even if he is killed, the radio is saved.

By noon of the second day, which was the first full day of hiking, they had crossed the border north of Achan and started to circle around it, heading, through a combination of primary jungle and *belukar*, for the swamps that lay between it and the River Koemba. The primary jungle was tolerable, if not exactly an easy hike, but the *belukar*, having been cleared and grown again, more dense than ever, required backbreaking work with the *parangs* and great patience.

Once they had to scatter to avoid the charge of a wild pig. Another time they had to move off the only track they had found for hours and circle around it, through even worse *belukar*, because a giant king cobra was coiled in the middle of the track and rose up hissing, preparing to attack, each time they tried to approach it. This simple detour cost them another hour, though it certainly saved lives.

That evening, when they lay up in their latest LUP, their poncho tents close together to discourage animal intrusions, Pete and Alf discussed the snake at great length, comparing it with similar reptiles they had seen in Malaya, and grossly exaggerating their recollections for the sake of young Terry.

'Snakes 20 feet long they had there,' Pete said with relish. 'They sting their victims, paralysing them but leaving them fully conscious, then swallow the poor fuckers whole.'

'I don't believe that,' Terry said.

'It's true,' Alf told him. 'Cross my heart, hope to die. A snake 30 feet long swallowed one of our mates and we could see the poor sod struggling inside its body, kicking and punching frantically, before that bastard finally digested him.'

'I can't see how a snake could digest a fully grown man,' Terry said rationally, determined not to be sent up, 'when he's kicking and punching its insides. That doesn't make sense.'

'They say it's got acids in its stomach that just melt you down,' Pete explained. 'A dreadful way to die, that.'

'You two should have been novelists,' Dead-eye said quietly. 'You both invent such wonderful stories.'

'Right,' Terry said. 'It's all bullshit.'

'You be cynical, then,' Alf said. 'Just choose to ignore us. But if one of them king cobras gets near you, you'll soon know different, kid.'

'You'll be swallowed whole, paralysed, fully conscious,' Pete solemnly informed him, 'then dissolved in its stomach juices. You won't sneer at us then!'

But Terry had rolled over in his sleeping bag and

was pretending to sleep. When eventually he did fall asleep, he had very bad dreams.

Luckily for Terry, given the horror of his dreams, he had to rise with the others at dawn and begin another day's march. An hour after setting off they stopped for breakfast. It was cold and unsatisfying. Four hours later they stopped for a late lunch that was not much better. To frustrate them even more, no one could 'honk', because now that they were deep in enemy territory, they were only allowed to speak – and then only in whispers – at night, in their isolated, hidden LUPs, while they were forcing down their awful grub. So after finishing this dismal cold lunch, they marched on again.

They had hiked for no more than an hour, through dense primary jungle, when Dead-eye heard the sound of axe blows up ahead. Signalling silently with his hand, he stopped the three men marching behind him. When they had all dropped to one knee with their weapons at the ready, Dead-eye listened intently. He heard the sound of axes on wood, then the faint murmur of distant voices speaking Malay. Indicating with another hand signal that the rest of the group should remain where they were, he slipped out of his bergen, uncocked his SLR and advanced at the crouch, weaving as quietly as possible from tree to tree, stopping when he could see exactly where the noises were coming from.

About 20 yards away, visible in a fragmented way through irregular windows in the undergrowth, a few Indonesian soldiers were at work, chopping down saplings and smaller trees. Out of sight, though heard distinctly, were many more men, maybe a whole platoon, clearly busy making jungle shelters.

Instinctively, Dead-eye started raising his rifle to the firing position, then realized what he was doing and lowered it again. His mission was to get to Seluas and attack Indonesian supply boats, not to engage the enemy in the jungle, let alone tackle a much larger force, which could be suicidal. Reminding himself of this, he turned around and headed back where he had come from.

The other men were still kneeling where he had left them, watching him intently. Using hand signals – one to say 'Enemy ahead', the other 'Follow me' – Dead-eye led them in a wide detour, avoiding the clearer passages through primary jungle, edging as quietly as humanly possible into an area of chest-high tropical ferns and an undergrowth filled with large, sharp-edged palm leaves and thorny bushes. As they went, they all took particular care lest signs of their passing – awkwardly bent fern stems, upside-down leaves, or even threads from their uniforms – should be noticed by any patrol from the enemy platoon. Thus it took the rest of that day to cover a mere three miles towards their objective.

By noon the next day they had reached a broad track running north-west from Poeri and almost certainly used regularly by soldiers going to Achan. Checking the actual track against his much-folded map, Dead-eye recognized it on the map from the faint blurs with which he had marked it and which he alone could see. In line with SAS thinking, he had not plastered his map with chinograph symbols indicating key points. He had also deliberately folded the map much more than necessary to prevent the enemy, if capturing it, from guessing which section had been used, as this in turn would have indicated to the enemy his main area of interest.

Satisfied that the track was clear, the men crossed it swiftly and vanished again into the *ulu*, now heading on a direct line for the swamps that led east to the River Koemba.

That afternoon they came to a recently cleared track running compass-true parallel to the river – so straight, in fact, that it would not only give a cut-off party a quick route to some border ambush, but also provide a devastating line of fire for enemy machine-guns.

Dead-eye silently indicated that Alf should photograph this particular part of the track from a few different angles. When Alf had done so, then written down the details of the location in his notebook, they crossed the track unnoticed. Even so, they were uncomfortably aware that in such a clearing there was always the possibility that the occupant of some unseen observation post had spotted them and, even worse, radioed in patrols to block their routes of advance and retreat.

In the event, no patrols appeared – nor were they likely to – for not too far ahead, just beyond some bamboo screens and a tangle of *belukar*, stretching away as far as the eye could see, was the dreaded swamp.

12

Knowing that it would be suicidal to enter the swamp at night, they searched around its edge for a suitable hide. Finding one, they quickly made up their bashas, trying to beat the sinking sun, rolling their sleeping bags out on leaves scattered under ponchos strung to the lower branches of the trees, stretched taut at an angle of 45 degrees, and fixed to the ground with rope and pegs.

Before supper could be enjoyed, Terry had to transmit Dead-eye's daily report back to Major Callaghan at SAS HQ, Pete had to check his explosives and Alf had to carefully annotate all the rolls of film he had shot so far. The sun was still sinking when each man quickly checked his rifle, removing the mud, twigs, leaves and even cobwebs that might have got into it; oiling the bolt, trigger mechanism and other moving parts; then rewrapping it in its jungle-coloured camouflage. They had to do all this before the sun sank, leaving them in complete darkness.

As they ate their cold supper of tinned sardines, biscuits and water, battling every second to keep off the flies, midges and mosquitoes, the sun set as a great ball of crimson-yellow lava behind the mountains west of the River Koemba. The lower it sank, the more it spread out along the alluvial top of the wooded mountains, until it resembled a great urn turned on its side and pouring molten metal which, hitting the mountain top, flooded north and south along its black summit. When the sun finally disappeared, vast clusters of opulent stars appeared over the soft peaks. Within minutes, however, those stars had been blotted out by gathering clouds darker than the sky and pregnant with rain.

In the event, the storm did not reach the SAS hide, though it created a magnificent *son et lumière* spectacle of light and sound. Fingers of lightning – accompanied by impressive rolls of thunder – clawed through boiling clouds, illuminating them from within with a magical radiance, and causing the stars to disappear and reappear in the pitch-black sky.

The storm went on for a long time, as if the jungle was exploding, yet there, near the swamp, from where they were seeing it so clearly, the SAS men felt it only in the form of teasing gusts of wind and a gradual lowering of temperature from the day's fierce heat to severe cold. Such cold they would have felt in any event with the coming of night.

The next morning, at dawn, with tendrils of mist hanging over the jungle and clinging like mournful ghosts to the tree trunks, the men broke up the hide, carefully hiding all traces of their presence, then embarked on the usual hour-long, pre-breakfast hike.

Moving into the swamp from north-east of the river bend, they quickly found themselves knee-deep in slimy, debris-covered water and assailed by madly buzzing insects. Though the bed of the swamp was soft and yielding – a combination of mud and small stones, dangerously cluttered with larger stones, fallen branches and other debris – they were able to push on towards Dead-eye's spur until, in the early afternoon, the water became too deep to cross and the mud too soft to walk on, particularly when carrying 50lb of bergen and 11lb of loaded SLR.

In this area gigantic bright-green palm leaves floated on the swamp and lay on small islands of firm ground, covered with seedlings and brown leaves. Surprisingly hard, they split if stepped on, giving off a loud crack that could have drawn attention to the wading men. For this reason, the men tried avoiding them, but even when they were pushed gently aside in the water, they often split with what seemed in the stillness a very loud noise, like a distant pistol shot.

'These leaves will do for us,' Pete whispered. 'They'll have the Indos all over us.'

'I think you're right,' Dead-eye replied. 'Let's call a halt for a moment.'

Leaning against the hard earth of one of the many small dry islands, though still waist-deep in water, the men wiped sweat from their faces, waved the swarms of flies and mosquitoes away, burned the leeches off their skin with cigarettes, and tried to catch their breath and relax in general.

'Dump your bergens on that dry ground behind you,' Dead-eye told the others. 'Might as well relax properly.' He waited until they had done so, then said: 'I don't see any point in all of us going on until we know exactly what's ahead. The maps don't help us here. There are no markings for the swamp. All I've got to go on is the general direction, but that doesn't tell me where we are now or how far away the river is. This water is getting deeper. The mud is getting thicker. If Terry slips, or simply sinks too deep in water, the radio will get damaged and we'll lose touch with HQ. Also, if present indications are anything to go by, this swamp will get worse the further south we go and we may find we have to dump the bergens. Without them we'll be lost, so I suggest that we keep them here, with two of us watching them and the other two advancing into the swamp to try finding that river.'

'Seems sensible,' Alf said.

'I agree,' Pete said.

'What about you?' Dead-eye asked Terry, taking him by surprise, but making him blush with pleasure.

'I agree as well,' he said. 'I'm getting worried about the radio. Wading here is like walking on quicksand and it's getting more dangerous. Your plan sounds good to me.'

'Good,' Dead-eye said. 'So you stay behind with the radio. As Alf's our medical specialist and photographer, he can stay here as well. Pete and I will leave our bergens here with you and go on without them. While we're gone, I want you to contact HQ every night and give them some kind of report – if only to tell them that we're still exploring the region. If we're not back within three days, assume we're casualties and return to the RV. Any questions?'

'No, boss.'

'Ok, Pete, let's go.'

Having already dumped their bergens on the small, dry island, Dead-eye and Pete started wading away from the others. Before disappearing around a screen of bamboo, they glanced back to see Alf and Terry clambering gratefully up onto the island.

Practically swimming, but holding their weapons above their heads, they headed south-east, hoping to catch a glimpse of the river and calculate where they were. They waded for a long time and saw nothing but more swamp, and when the sun started sinking they both realized that they could be in danger in more ways than one.

In fact, they were in a frightening position, for they had only one spare magazine apiece, plus their *parangs* and escape kit. This would not help them much if they could not find their way back through the tangle of rank vegetation in the late afternoon's fading light.

As Dead-eye and Pete waded forward, the latter distanced himself from the former to reduce their chances of being killed by a single burst of gunfire. This could well happen. The water, as Dead-eye noticed, was swishing quietly past them, leaving a tell-tale trail across the surface scum. An enemy soldier could follow that watery trail right to its source and blow their brains out.

Dead-eye knew the risks and did not give in to fear, instead giving most of his concentration to his compass and the rest to his wading, making sure that each footstep among the submerged tangle of roots was reasonably secure. To break an ankle here would be a disaster, possibly fatal.

Following Dead-eye, Pete was both fascinated

and repelled by the sight of slimy marsh bugs racing on their numerous legs across the weed-covered surface. Magnified, he realized, they would look horrible. The thought made him shiver.

Just before darkness fell, they clambered onto a small strip of dry land under a natural umbrella of large palm fronds, where they laid up for the night, first having a basic snack of blocks of dry meat washed down with water. They slept as best they could beneath the overhanging palms, surrounded by the scum-covered swamp, numbed by the cold, tormented by numerous, unseen creepy-crawlies, to wake black and blue from insect bites.

'We've been eaten alive,' Pete whispered grimly, studying the bites and stings on his arms and chest. 'We've probably picked up every disease known to man – and some unique to this swamp. Fuck this for a lark, boss.'

'Keep your voice down,' Dead-eye whispered. 'We still don't know what's out there.'

'We don't even know where we are,' Pete whispered even softer than before. 'We're just wandering blind.'

'No, we're not,' Dead-eye told him, checking his compass. 'The map may be useless, but at least we know the river's south, and according to this compass that's where we're heading, so let's keep going, Corporal.'

'Anything you say, boss.'

For the rest of that day they roamed on a south-easterly arc across the swamp, trying to find the River Koemba. Failing, they grew frustrated and discussed heading back to the others. But then, just as they did so, they heard the heavy throb of diesel engines, coming from no more than two or three miles further south.

'That's it,' Dead-eye said. 'That's the sound of a supply boat. It can only be travelling along the River Koemba. That's where we have to go.'

'Are you sure, boss?'

'Yes, Pete, I'm sure. And it can't be too far away.'

Yet even though they waded south-east for another hour, they saw nothing beyond an almost solid wall of bamboo and tall reeds, thrusting up from water so deep and muddy that it could not be crossed.

'Fuck it,' Dead-eye said, even as he heard the throb of another diesel engine in the distance, beyond that impenetrable wall of tightly tangled bamboo and reeds. 'There has to be another way. Let's backtrack north-west to the firm ground where we left the others. They must be getting lonely by now.'

They managed to make it back to the others before last light the same day. That night, making themselves as comfortable as best they could on the same small island, the four men had a 'Chinese parliament' to pool suggestions. Out of this came the simple plan to continue south-east, following the line of the River Sentimo until they reached the River Koemba. They could then follow the latter due east until it took them to Seluas.

Having agreed on that, they all sighed with relief, then turned into their bashas to endure another night as best they could in a nightmare of whining insects, stinging creepy-crawlies, and unseen birds and animals that only made their presence noisily known when a man was trying to sleep.

They felt like hell the next morning.

13

As agreed, they moved out early the next day, heading south, wading waist-deep in the water for what seemed like an eternity, though it actually took them only three miles, to the confluence of the Rivers Poeteh and Sentimo. As Dead-eye had predicted, the water here was deeper, the foliage more impenetrable, but when they tried following the river, wading through even worse swamps, they soon lost it in dense jungle. Doggedly wading on, they found themselves emerging to relatively clear, swampy land which Dead-eye predicted was due north of the River Koemba.

Pressing on, they came to a series of slow-flowing tributaries that wound their way between a maze of dry banks and curtains of bamboo. They were trying to cross this maze, up to their waists in water, when a large boat, judging by the sound of its engine, swished by on the other side of a high bamboo curtain. Its wash lifted the flotsam of leaves so high that Alf was practically submerged, though he managed to hold his SLR above his head until he had surfaced again, spitting water and weeds from his mouth, then cursing angrily.

No one ribbed him; they dared not speak. Unable to see through the curtain of bamboo, beyond which was the channel along which the boat had passed, Dead-eye decided to change direction and head back into the swamp to avoid accidentally emerging into the river just as another boat was passing.

The change of direction turned out to be the SAS men's first lucky break, since after wading for another four hours, hidden in the swamp but following the line of the river, they reached firm ground. It was, Dead-eye was convinced from its appearance, the fingertip of the spur he had been seeking.

'No doubt about it,' he said, checking his map against a compass reading. 'This is the spur.'

Pleased, Dead-eye put the map and compass away, then took in the scene as they knelt on the edge of the narrow strip of dry jungle, hidden by tall grass, looking at the broad sweep of the River Koebma where it curved around the well-spaced trees of a rubber plantation. On his left the strip of jungle continued right up to the river bank. He pointed to it with his forefinger. 'That could make an OP.'

He was right: it was just right for an observation post. In the centre of the strip of dry jungle a large tree spread its branches above dense scrub and a shallow ditch, but with open ground surrounding both – as open as it was to his right, where the rows of rubber trees spread along the river bank. The trees were being 'rested', with no sign of recent tappings, though Dead-eye saw that there were some well-used paths through the plantation, indicating that it was still being worked.

As a site for their OP, Dead-eye plumped for the lone tree and its scrub-covered, shallow ditch. Feeling exposed where he was kneeling, and having made sure that there were no enemy troops in the immediate vicinity, he ordered the patrol into the scrub surrounding and covering the ditch.

'Make four scrapes under the scrub,' he said. 'Two men facing the river, two facing the jungle. And be quick about it.'

'Anything for a kip,' Alf said. 'Even building an OP.'

'A little home from home,' Pete added, 'with a view of the river.'

'Shut up and start scraping.'

'Yes, boss!' they both chimed.

The simple OP was made up by digging four shallow depressions in the soft earth for their bashas – two facing the river for the purposes of observation, the others facing the jungle behind: one for observation, the second for sleeping in, with one man sleeping at a time. The scrapes were filled with a bed of leaves and the sleeping bags were then rolled out on the leaves. Another shallow scrape, placed in the centre of the four larger ones, was used as a well for kit and weapons. To help keep out the rain, ponchos were raised on forked sticks above the scrapes and pegged to the ground. The scrub was pulled closely over the ponchos and in turn covered with more leaves and foliage. Narrow 'windows' were made to the front and back of the foliage to give the men an adequate view of the river and jungle.

When the OP was completed, they settled down to wait, though they did not waste their time while doing so. Dead-eye updated his logbook and also redrew his map in the light of his recent explorations through the swamp, marking accessible routes, good lying-up positions, and average time-to-distance figures for the various routes recommended. Alf photographed the river and any traffic on it, whether civilian or military, and made notes on the shots he was taking, including the date, the time of day and a written description of the contents of the passing traffic and the direction in which it was cruising. Terry, as well as acting as the sentry facing the jungle behind the OP, checked through the various wavebands of his radio in hopes of picking up enemy transmissions as well as encoded news of other SAS patrols. Last but not least, Pete kept his eye on the river and his SLR aimed and ready to fire. His specialist skill, demolition, was of no use here.

They had not been in the OP for long when the first military launch chugged past, crewed by six half-naked Dyaks. Two uniformed Indonesian soldiers were sitting on the deck with their legs outstretched and their backs resting against tarpaulin-covered supplies. Their idea of protecting the cargo was to idly watch the river bank slip by. The boat flew the red-and-white ensign of Indonesia.

'Let's finish them off,' Pete whispered.

'No,' Dead-eye replied. 'First, we have to spend a few days just watching, photographing and taking notes on the traffic to establish just how much of it there is. We need permission from HQ to attack, and that'll only be received when we're ready to bug out.'

'Shit!' Pete whispered in frustration, then rolled away from the window in the foliage and said to Alf: 'It's all yours, mate.'

Alf immediately took his mate's position and began to take photos of the passing launch. When he had done so, he quickly jotted down as many of its details as he could manage before it disappeared from view.

No other military craft passed that afternoon. By nightfall the SAS men had to fight a combination of boredom and exhaustion. Once darkness fell, however, they were able to slip down to the water's edge to fill the large communal bottle, as well as their personal canisters. They purified the water with tablets before drinking it. Supper was a choice between dehydrated meat and tinned sardines, supplemented for some with cheese. Dead-eye spiced his sardines with curry powder, the smell of which nauseated the other three, who said it was putting them off their desserts of chocolate or sweets.

Finally, before settling down for the night, Terry transmitted, encoded, Dead-eye's daily report to HQ. Receiving an acknowledgement, he was reminded that the real world still existed. But for now he was in this alien, unreal world, the light fading, the river gurgling in front of him, the jungle whispering behind him, the nocturnal chorus of the birds and animals steadily rising in the trees to deprive him and the others of sleep.

In fact, they all slept well that night, waking refreshed.

Shortly after a breakfast of oatmeal blocks washed down with cold tea, they had a bit of a scare when two Indonesian soldiers appeared around the bend in the river and paddled up to a tree on the bank, very close to the OP. Wondering if this seemingly innocent act was in fact a diversionary move to cover an attack on the OP across the open ground behind it, Dead-eye decided to take no chances and ordered his men to adopt firing positions front and rear, cautioning them not to shake the scrub as they did so.

Rolling belly-down into the scrapes and gently easing the barrels of their SLRs through the scrub, the men took aim. Dead-eye and Pete covered the men in the boat; the other two covered the jungle behind the OP.

They lay like that for some time, not moving, hardly breathing. Though it seemed like an eternity, it was, in reality, only the few minutes it took for the Indonesian soldiers in the boat to empty a fish trap and go back down the river, rowing casually and chatting and laughing in loud, high voices.

'They don't seem too concerned about being overheard,' Pete observed.

'A good sign,' Dead-eye replied. 'That means they don't suspect we're in the area. They've just made my day.'

The rest of the day was equally busy, with a little local traffic in the morning followed by a greater number of military supply boats flying the Indonesian flag and manned by armed troops. Obviously they were cruising to and from the trading settlement at Seluas, which Dead-eye estimated was about five miles downstream.

With so much traffic passing, Alf was kept busy with his camera, and Pete had to take over the job of entering details of the traffic in the logbook. So busy were they that they had no time for lunch.

By early afternoon, with the sun high in the sky, the OP was intoleraby hot, full of buzzing flies and whining mosquitoes, and smelt of sweat and piss. Unable to leave their cover, the men urinated and defecated into plastic bags, in full view of each other, then sealed the bags and buried them in the mud. To make them even more uncomfortable, ants were hurrying back and forth in long lines across the bottom of the ditch, invading the kit well and crawling over food and weapons alike.

Even worse, spiders the size of an outspread hand occasionally emerged from holes in the mud and clambered fearlessly over the men's boots. Unsettled though the men were by the experience, they had to resist the impulse to violently kick or swipe the giant spiders off, since this would have disturbed the foliage, possibly attracting the attention of the armed sentries on the Indonesian launches passing by less than 20 yards away. Instead, the harmless, though hideous spiders had to be removed with a gentle brush of the hand, which meant touching them longer than the men would have liked.

Terry, in particular, poured sweat each time a spider crawled over his booted foot or trouser leg. He shuddered each time he had to perform the ghastly task of brushing it off.

'Are you all right?' Dead-eye asked, obviously concerned.

'Yes, Sarge, I'm OK.'

'Are you sure?'

'Yes. They just give me the willies.'

'They're harmless.'

'They still give me the willies, but I'm all right.'

'Good. Stick it out, Trooper.'

By late afternoon the SAS men were growing frustrated at their inability to attack the passing supply boats. Their frustration was increased by the sheer number of vessels on the river, most of them piled high with supplies for the Indonesian battalions.

Just before dusk, as storm clouds were gathering over the jungle canopy and great striations of light were streaming across the dimming sky, the men's frustration dissolved into an almost hallucinatory state of disbelief as a large, immaculate cruising yacht approached around the bend in the river, passing only fifteen yards from the men.

As the vessel approached, a beautiful Indonesian girl in a white swimsuit stepped out of the deckhouse, draping a bathing towel over one arm. With shapely legs, full breasts, a flawless, high-cheekboned face, and long, ebony hair cascading down to the small of her back, she was a rare, unexpected vision of loveliness who took each man's breath away.

After walking along the side of the yacht, ignoring the helpless, nervous stares of the Indonesian sentries, she spread out the towel on the deck, put on a pair of sunglasses, then stretched out on her back on the towel, raising an elegant leg and turning her face to the side. She lay there, frozen in crimson twilight, as the yacht passed the SAS men, so close that its wash splashed over the bank just below the OP.

'I don't believe it!' Pete whispered.

'Christ, she's beautiful!' Terry murmured.

'She isn't sunbathing. She's just cooling down,' Pete fantasized. 'She must have worked up a sweat in that cabin with some fat-bellied bastard.'

'I'm coming just thinking about it,' Alf informed them, then released a soft, melodramatic groan. 'Oh, God help me!'

'Forget the girl,' Dead-eye said in his more

pragmatic way. 'That boat makes a great target. It obviously belongs to a high-ranking civilian official – not a military officer.'

'Military officers don't get women like that,' Pete said as the yacht passed. 'That's some wonderful whore, boss.'

'It could have been his daughter,' Terry said, his face filled with yearning as the vessel moved on and the girl disappeared out of sight behind the bulwark.

Alf rolled his eyes, then shook his head in disbelief. 'Innocence is surely bliss!' he exclaimed. 'His *daughter*, for God's sake!'

'Quieten down, you men,' Dead-eye growled. 'The way you're talking, you might as well get a megaphone and announce our presence up and down the river. We're here to recce that river, not ogle corrupt local officials' bints. Now let's get back to business.'

After another minute or so of moans, groans and excited whispers, the men quietened down and went back to their work.

The sun started sinking. Darkness crept across the jungle. Lightning flashed through the dark clouds in the distant sky, followed by thunder.

Twenty minutes passed. Another launch came along the river with seven soldiers spread carelessly under its fixed canopy, eating and smoking in an unconcerned manner. Alf took the last photograph of the day and Pete logged the details. Then darkness fell.

'Day's work done,' Alf whispered, removing the roll of film from his camera.

'A lot of traffic in this little logbook,' Pete informed them. 'It certainly wasn't time wasted.'

'That girl was gorgeous,' Terry reminded them. '*That's* why the time wasn't wasted. I'd lie here for another couple of days just to see her again.'

'He's a romantic,' Alf said.

'For lithesome whores,' Pete corrected him.

'You don't have to be sarcastic,' Terry said. 'I'm just saying she was gorgeous to look at. No harm in that.'

'Shut up!' snapped Dead-eye in a hoarse whisper, glancing up and down the dark river, clearly frustrated. 'I've had enough of this. Get on that A41, Terry, and tell those bastards at HQ that Sergeant Parker requests permission to fire on any suitable target, starting tomorrow. You get that? *Now do it!*'

Terry transmitted the message and they all sat back and waited, gorging on their personal preference among tinned sardines, blocks of dehydrated meat, cheese, dry biscuits, chocolate, sweets, cold tea and plain water. Though Alf and Pete were gasping for cigarettes, Dead-eye refused to let them light up lest the glow be seen by the enemy.

Forty minutes later, when the distant electrical storm had arrived at the river and was pouring rain on the OP to the accompaniment of thunder and lightning, Terry received a transmission from HQ granting immediate permission to attack suitable targets.

If the men had been allowed to make a sound, they would have leapt up and cheered.

14

Now that they could attack suitable targets, the men felt more enthusiastic when they woke the next morning. Shortly after completing their usual dismal breakfast, they saw two Indonesian soldiers passing by in a canoe with their Lee-Enfield .303-inch bolt-action rifles lying on the crossboard between them. While they could have been snatched as useful prisoners, Dead-eye refused the men permission to do so, insisting that sinking a launch would be much more effective.

'Apart from depriving the Indos of supplies,' he explained, 'the loss of a whole boat might frighten the river community into not cooperating with them in general.'

'The other side of the hearts-and-minds coin,' Terry said.

'Thanks a million for that clarification, Mr Einstein,' Pete said.

'It's good to have a brilliant tactician in the

OP with you,' Alf added. 'Sort of fills you with confidence.'

'Just kill the sarcasm, you two,' Dead-eye told them. 'And as a matter of fact, Terry's right. He knows more than you two arseholes put together.' Then suddenly his voice dropped to a whisper: 'Keep your voices down. That canoe's coming closer.'

The two soldiers in the canoe rowed right past the OP, hardly glancing at the high banks, both apparently lost in their thoughts as they studied the river. If it had not been for their uniforms and the rifles lying between them, they would have seemed like two men on a fishing trip. They rowed slowly, lazily, as if they had all day, and eventually disappeared around the bend where the river turned due east.

'They'll never know how lucky they were,' Terry whispered.

'Luck has a way of running out,' Dead-eye replied in his soft but oddly chilling manner. 'Their day might yet come.'

A longboat with a thatched canopy followed shortly after, poled by half-naked, colourfully tattooed Ibans, who were helped by the swiftly flowing current pushing them downstream. This was followed by another canoe, also rowed by Ibans; then by a couple of motor launches crewed by Iban traders and piled high with supplies for their kampongs. After that, for the next five hours, only the usual small boats passed the OP, some carrying Indonesian soldiers, but most not.

As the day wore on, the men grew impatient and started begging Dead-eye to let them make a strike.

'You said any suitable target,' Pete reminded him, 'and these are suitable targets, boss.'

'No, they're not,' Dead-eye insisted. 'They're mostly just locals. When we *have* seen Indo soldiers, they've been in boats too small to bother with. We need something bigger.'

'How big, for Christ's sake?' Alf was close to the limit of his patience. 'The *Ark Royal* won't be coming along, so let's settle for something less.'

'We can't hit anything less,' Dead-eye told him. 'We'll only get one shot at it. Once we mount an attack, the word will go up and down the river and we'll have to clear out of here. So the first one is the last one and it has to be worthwhile. That's why we have to be patient and wait for the right one. Understood?'

Alf sighed. 'Yes, boss.'

Nevertheless, his frustration was almost palpable, as was that of the others. The enthusiasm with which they had greeted the dawn began to disappear and was in no way improved when the rising heat brought back the flies and mosquitoes, the stench of sweat and piss, and the huge spiders that emerged from the mud to crawl relentlessly over them.

Nor did their mood lighten when the afternoon rain clouds darkened the sky and suddenly burst over them, the rain making a deafening drumming sound on the camouflaged ponchos and hitting the palm leaves so hard that they quivered rhythmically and, in some cases, were torn from their stems. So heavy was the rain that it flooded the ponchos and made them sag with the weight of water, which then poured off the edges of the ponchos and down into the OP. More water poured in from the surrounding earth and gradually flooded the ditch where Alf and Terry were lying belly-down, trying to watch the jungle.

'It's covering us!' Alf complained. 'We'll soon have to sit up. We'll probably have to get out of here.'

'It's already up to my nose and rising damned quickly,' confirmed Terry.

Though Dead-eye and Pete were kneeling at the front of the OP, to get a good view through the windows, the water was rising there, too, and already washing around their boots.

'The whole OP's flooding. We'll have to evacuate,' Pete said to Dead-eye.

'Damn!' Dead-eye muttered.

At that precise moment, above the roar of thunder and the fearsome crack of lightning, he heard the distant chugging of what sounded like a large launch approaching through the downpour.

Wiping the rain from his eyes and looking up in disbelief, Dead-eye saw what was indeed a very large motor launch coming upriver around the western bend. When it had rounded the bend and was approaching him, he saw that it was crowded with enemy soldiers and piled high with supplies.

'Perfect!' he exclaimed, not bothering any longer to whisper, since no one other than those with him in the OP could hear him. 'Just what I was waiting for.'

'I'm drowning!' Terry shouted, trying to keep his face out of the water rising rapidly in the ditch.

'Get up, you stupid prat,' Pete told him. 'What the fuck are you doing down there? Playing with your toy submarine?'

Terry rolled onto his back, then quickly sat upright, shaking the water off him like a dog as Alf, also grateful to get out of the rising water, slithered up the muddy side of the ditch and stared over the river.

'Wow!' Alf exclaimed softly, seeing the boat for the first time. 'What a fucking beauty!'

The big launch was now coming level with the

OP, allowing them to get a good look at its cargo, as well as the men milling about on deck. The men were all fully uniformed soldiers and the cargo was mostly in large wooden crates, suggesting weapons and ammunition. The rain obscured other details.

'I've got to get a picture of this,' Alf said, removing the camera from his bergen, where he had stowed it to protect it from the rain. '*If* I can get one in this light.'

'Then be quick about it,' Dead-eye said. 'It'll pass any moment now.' While Alf was frantically snapping away, not expecting good results, Dead-eye was squinting through the rain at the approaching boat. 'Ok,' he said as he checked his rifle, then uncocked it and switched to automatic fire. 'It's a shoot-and-scoot job. We wait until she's passing the OP – right there in front of us – then we rake her from prow to stern. The intention is not only to finish off the troops, but also to smash the boat to hell. When she's passed – or when what's left of her has passed – we bug out and don't look back. Now go to it, men.'

As the launch approached, the rain was lashing down so hard that the drops bounced off its cabin roof as well as off the river's rushing surface, where it formed a dazzling silvery tapestry. The canvas side screens of the cabin were closed against the storm, but Dead-eye knew that there were more men behind them, most of them officers.

Them and their whores, he thought cynically. But that's not my concern.

Having come up from the ditch, Alf and Terry spaced themselves about eight feet apart, one either side of Pete. Dead-eye then moved to direct the fire-fight from their left, on slightly lower ground that was covered by the water pouring noisily into the OP. From there, though ankle-deep in water and pounded by the rain, he had a clear view of the river as it swung downstream to the right, flowing to the south-east, past the Indonesians' trading settlement at Seluas.

As the launch drew level with the OP and then passed it like a great whale strung with glowing oil lamps obscured by the heavy rain, the rest of the men checked their weapons, cocked them, switched to automatic fire, then braced themselves and took aim.

'The rest of you fire when I do,' Dead-eye told them, squinting along the sights of his SLR.

He saw the prow of the launch through his night-vision sight, with the enemy soldiers gathered near it, staring along the river, some shielding their eyes against the rain with cupped hands, others huddled under their ponchos, playfully punching one another and giggling. Other men, the heavily armed crack troops, were, like their officers, hidden by canvas screens over the open deck near the stern.

The prow slipped out of view and the main deck appeared, packed with soldiers huddled around the piles of crates, most leaning against the tarpaulins, with their ponchos wrapped tightly about them to keep out the rain. That picture also moved on, slipping out of sight, ghostlike in the eerie green glow of Dead-eye's night-vision sight.

Then the bulwark came into view, in the dead centre of his sight, with more soldiers, obviously officers, standing near the steering wheel and pointing at the jungle, where the thunder was rumbling and the lightning was daggering through black clouds. They were obviously concerned more about the storm than anything else, which was fine by Dead-eye.

He got one officer dead in his sights, then pressed the trigger of his SLR, which roared in his right ear. The officer went into a convulsion, frantically throwing up his arms, then spun backwards, almost somersaulting, and fell out of sight.

Dead-eye kept firing as the bulwark moved on and was replaced with the stern. By this time Pete, Alf and Terry had also opened fire and the boat, while slipping past his line of vision, was turned into a hell of exploding wood, flying shards of smashed glass, running, ducking, falling, screaming men, and expanding, dazzling balls of fire from exploding oil lamps.

Within the space of thirty seconds Alf and Terry had each put their full twenty rounds into the launch, one magazine full, just as Dead-eye had ordered. Dead-eye had added fifteen rounds of his own and Pete had fired half a magazine before Dead-eye called 'Stop!'

All four immediately reloaded with a full magazine, as was the standard drill. Though he had half a magazine left, Pete did the same because he did not want to be caught in another action with only ten rounds.

When Dead-eye opened fire again, the rest followed suit.

While Dead-eye continued taking out the soldiers still on deck, Alf and Terry hammered away at the launch's waterline, hoping to either tear it to shreds or put enough bullets into it to flood it and sink it.

Meanwhile, Pete's SLR jammed. Cursing, he checked the weapon and cleared the stoppage in seconds. He began firing again as some of the soldiers, who had been laughing happily just a few seconds before, were set on fire by the burning oil from the exploded lamps and threw themselves screaming over the side of the boat, preferring to drown rather than burn to death.

By now the sustained fire aimed at the waterline had begun to have its desired effect and the launch had begun to list, with flames dancing up from the spilled oil blazing on the decks, black smoke billowing up and blowing backwards on the wind, and burning men pushing aside the canvas screens to jump over the side. Splashing into the river, which was now torrential because of the torrential rain, they were either swept downstream, fighting to stay afloat, or smashed into the high, muddy banks, where they were knocked unconscious and sank.

Smoke hung low in the heavy rain as it spread from beneath the canvas screens now flapping loose on the deck of the burning, listing, sinking launch.

Knowing that the boat's signaller had almost certainly transmitted an alarm call as soon as he heard the firing, and not wanting to be around when enemy choppers arrived to rake the vicinity with their guns or deposit troops sent to find the SAS ambush party, Dead-eye stopped firing and waved at Alf and Terry to withdraw.

After locking their SLRs and slinging them over their shoulders, Alf and Terry picked up their bergens, strapped them to their backs, then made a dash for the rubber trees, covered by Dead-eye and Pete, who watched the river, blinking repeatedly and squinting into the rain to check that no enemy patrols were coming along the bank.

Once in the relative safety of the jungle, Alf and Terry adopted firing positions, ready to give covering fire if any Indonesians appeared, while Dead-eye and Pete clambered out of the flooded, muddy OP and ran for the trees.

Suddenly, Dead-eye darted back to the ditch.

'What the fuck . . .?' Imagining that Dead-eye had seen enemy riflemen in the plantations, Pete, as number two, followed him back to the OP. Dead-eye, however, had only gone back to retrieve the large communal water bottle.

'We've a long way to go,' he explained, 'Besides, we don't want to leave anything that might help the Indos identify us. That's it, Pete. Let's go.'

Glancing back at the river, they saw the Indonesian boat, now listing heavily and on fire from prow to stern, sinking into the river, while the soldiers still alive were either burnt to death in the blazing oil slicks spreading out from the sinking vessel or were swept away in the swift waters, now merely part of the debris.

Satisfied, Dead-eye led Pete back to Alf and Terry, then the four men fled into the jungle.

15

As they moved back into the *ulu*, Dead-eye and the others saw the light of an explosion through the mist and rain, flaring up over the river and the rubber plantation, indicating that the launch had rolled onto its side and was finally sinking.

'We did it,' Pete said. 'The fucker's gone down. We pulled it off, boys.'

'Which is exactly why we have to keep moving,' Dead-eye said. 'That boat will have sent out an SOS the minute we opened fire on it. The Indos are going to be on our tail, so we've no time to waste. Let's get the hell out of here.'

Burdened down with their bergens, they embarked on the short, difficult hike back over the maze of watery channels, dry banks and curtains of bamboo until they reached the southern tip of the swamp, bordered by a dense tangle of *belukar*. Forced to stoop down under the lower branches and palm leaves, they had an arduous trek for the next hour, their backs breaking and every muscle taut. It was therefore a relief when they could straighten up again and advance like human beings, even though each step took them deeper into the scum-covered water.

As Dead-eye led them along at a pace that showed no mercy, with each man distanced safely from the one ahead, a king cobra hidden in a branch about four feet above the water suddenly reared its large, plate-shaped hood and started hissing aggressively, ready to strike at Dead-eye's chest.

Almost as quick and as deadly as the snake, Dead-eye aimed his SLR at its swaying head, then froze motionless, holding the barrel absolutely steady, practically touching the snake's open, salivating jaws and darting forked tongue.

The rest of the men, spaced well apart behind Dead-eye, froze as well, not knowing why he had stopped.

Still standing there frozen, with the barrel of his SLR practically down the great snake's throat, Dead-eye did not know quite what to do. Certainly, he knew that to fire the rifle might give away his patrol's position.

Pete, standing a few yards behind him, knew this also, which explains why, though having seen the snake, he was aiming at it, but not actually firing. In fact, Pete was not only worried about a shot alerting the enemy. He was concerned that, since his two friends behind him could not see what was happening, they might think the shot was from an Indonesian patrol and therefore take the required evasive action, breaking away from the single-file formation and melting into the *ulu*, possibly to never be seen again.

So for those two reasons, though seeing the snake spitting and hissing only inches from Dead-eye's face, Pete could not bring himself to press the trigger.

As for Alf and Terry, neither knew why Dead-eye had stopped, so they prepared for any eventuality and were ready to fire.

Dead-eye did not move a muscle. He out-stared the hissing creature. Eventually, the snake, having no cause to strike the rock-still sergeant, retracted its hood, slid away and disappeared behind a log in the muddy ground.

Dead-eye heaved a sigh of relief. He hurried up to Pete, who shook his head in disbelief, then they both glanced back in the direction they had come from. Even here, a good half mile from the river, they could still smell the smoke and burning oil from the sinking launch.

'Let's go,' Dead-eye whispered.

They waded deeper into the swamp, forced as usual to endure the swarms of flies, mosquitoes

214

and midges, constantly alert for sea snakes, concentrating at all times on not breaking an ankle on one of the many large stones on the swamp bed, or losing balance by treading on an underwater log, or sinking or slipping in the clinging mud. Also forced as usual to carry their SLRs above their heads to keep them dry, they soon had badly aching muscles and sharp, stabbing pains between their shoulder blades.

This time, at least, Dead-eye was using a map annotated by himself from the previous journey, so he had only to retrace his own footsteps, as it were, to get them back to the RV on the other side of the border. The enemy, however, had other ideas.

The SAS men's first indication that they were being followed was when an Indonesian Army helicopter flew low overhead, obviously searching the swamp. Seeing it, they froze where they where, hoping that their camouflaged clothes would make them merge into the swamp and that their lack of movement would leave no rippling wake on the water that could be seen from above.

When the helicopter disappeared, the men moved on again, but less than twenty minutes later a second helicopter appeared, this time suddenly roaring out of the southern sky and hovering right above where they were wading through a stretch of swamp covered with tangled, obstructing vegetation. Holding their rifles up with one hand and hacking at the dense foliage with a *parang* held in the other, they were taken by surprise and had no time to freeze before the pilot saw them and brought the chopper down to hover right over them.

An enemy soldier was kneeling behind a machine-gun fixed to the floor at the open side door of the helicopter. When he saw the men struggling through the swamp, he opened fire on them. With the helicopter hovering dangerously close to the trees and swaying slightly from side to side, the gunner had difficulty in keeping his aim steady. His first burst therefore went wide, making the water boil violently some yards from the men. This gave them time to wade behind the nearest tree trunks, from where they were able to fire back with their SLRs switched to automatic. Instead of ascending, the chopper actually dropped lower to give the gunner a better view of his target.

Now Pete and Alf appreciated having the more powerful SLR, rather than the lighter Armalite, for they were able to put some bullets into the helicopter, stitching a line just above the door and hitting something inside that burst into flames.

Sucked out on the helicopter's own slipstream, the flames roared through the open door to engulf the unfortunate gunner, whose screams

were like nothing remotely human. As the helicopter ascended, still on fire and pouring smoke,
a crewman inside, attempting to put out the
flames, kicked out the blazing, screaming gunner.
He fell like a blazing projectile, kicking and
screaming, leaving a vertical stream of smoke
to mark his downward course, and was only
silenced when he plunged into the swamp a good
distance away. The helicopter turned around and
headed back the way it had come, still pouring
smoke.

'He'll tell the others where we are,' Dead-eye
said. 'Now they'll start coming after us. We'd better
make tracks.'

They continued wading through the swamp,
passing the dead pilot, whose charred, smouldering
body was sinking slowly, then heading deeper into
an area covered with overhanging *belukar*. When
another helicopter flew overhead, the *belukar* hid
them from view, but half an hour later they saw
another chopper behind them, this one a larger
transport, hovering low enough to enable a good
dozen troopers to climb down a rope ladder into
the swamp where the first pilot had seen them.

'Shit!' Dead-eye softly exclaimed. 'That's what I
feared. We'd better move faster.'

They continued their laborious, exhausting
advance through the swamp, now desperate to

get out of it and onto dry land, even if it was *belukar*, before the Indonesians caught up with them. Unfortunately, about fifteen minutes later, another transport helicopter flew overhead and deposited a second group of enemy troopers about a mile directly ahead of them.

'They know where we are,' Dead-eye said, 'and what direction we're heading in. They're going to cordon off the whole swamp and move in on all sides.'

Now it was Pete's turn to softly whisper, 'Shit!' He glanced about him, in every direction, as if expecting to see the enemy burst out of the undergrowth. 'What the fuck do we do?'

'We keep going,' Alf said. 'We don't have a choice. We can't go back and we can't detour, because no matter which way we go, we're going to have to fight our way out. So we might as well keep advancing.'

'I second that,' Terry said, also glancing about him, wondering just how fast their pursuers would close in.

'I agree,' Dead-eye said. 'We don't have a choice. If they're going to cordon off the whole swamp, we might as well keep going and be prepared for a fire-fight. At least the swamp from here on is relatively clear of dense undergrowth, so our hands will be free.' He held up his SLR to show them

218

what he meant. 'Be prepared,' he said. 'Release the safety-catch. OK, let's go.'

They marched without incident for about half an hour, then stopped when they heard movement ahead. Quickly taking up positions, each man behind a different tree, they waited until the foliage just ahead parted and the first man in an enemy patrol emerged, waist-deep in water, holding a Lee-Enfield .303 bolt-action rifle across his chest at an angle.

Relatively safe hidden in this lengthy stretch of *belukar*, Dead-eye did not want the sound of shots to give away their position. Working on the assumption that the lone soldier was a scout, out on point and well away from the main patrol, he gave a hand signal, indicating that no one should fire, then carefully slung his SLR by its strap over his left shoulder. With his right hand he withdrew his commando dagger from its sheath and pressed himself against the trunk of the tree, waiting for the soldier to pass him. He did so a few seconds later, his left shoulder actually brushing the branches around Dead-eye's face.

The Indonesian looked about eighteen and had large brown eyes and delicate features slightly marred by tension. Dead-eye saw the beads of sweat gleaming on his brown skin. Without taking a step – since the soldier would have heard the moving water – Dead-eye leaned forward, slapped his hand around his mouth, silencing him, then jerked his head back and swiftly drew the blade across his taut throat, slashing through to the windpipe. Blood shot out in a long, thin arc, squirting through Dead-eye's fingers, as the soldier released a strangled, gargling sound, convulsing and dropping his rifle. The weapon splashed into the water being kicked up by his convulsions. When the man was still, Dead-eye lowered him gently into the swamp, where his blood poured out, turning the water red.

Dead-eye cleaned his bloody left hand on some leaves, cleaned and sheathed the knife the same way, then removed his SLR from his shoulder and waved the others forward. Knowing that the rest of the enemy patrol would not be far ahead, they moved with particular care, stopping every few minutes to watch and listen. Their patience was rewarded when they heard the sound of movement directly ahead.

Spreading well out and melting back into the trees on either side of what they assumed would be the enemy's path, they were rewarded when the six-man patrol emerged from the foliage, wading carefully through the water, and passed by without noticing their presence.

The SAS men waited for five minutes to ensure

that the patrol was well out of earshot, then started to move on. But they were stopped by a hand signal from Pete.

When Dead-eye looked enquiringly at Pete, the latter walked up to the sergeant and whispered, 'Once those six Indos find the body of their dead scout, they'll turn back to get us. I think we should give them a little surprise.' When Dead-eye again stared at his number two, saying nothing, Pete grinned and removed a Claymore anti-tank land-mine from his bergen. 'I've been keeping this for a rainy day,' he whispered. 'Obviously I can't bury it in the ground, but I *can* put it up there as a booby-trap.' He pointed to the lower branches of the trees.

'Do it,' Dead-eye said.

Pete waded through the water, pushed the foliage aside, then clambered up to the lower branches of the nearest tree, checking carefully that there were no snakes sleeping up above. Sitting on the thickest branch, which was just above the surface of the plant-covered water, he tied one of the Claymores to its underside with the cord from his bergen, then attached a lengthy piece of trip-wire to it. Clambering down again, he let the trip-wire run out through his fingers as he waded across the route taken by the enemy patrol, which he treated as an imaginary 'path' about ten feet wide. He stopped at a tree well to the other side of the 'path'. After tying the wire to the tangled roots of the tree, he tugged it until it was tight enough to trip the mine if moved by the passage of a human body or leg. As the wire was just under the surface of the water it would not be seen by its potential victims.

'Job done,' he whispered, proudly surveying his handiwork.

'How many have you got?' Dead-eye asked him.

'Four.'

'Let's set the other three up the same way at intervals of about a mile. We've about three miles of swamp still to cover before reaching the *ulu* proper, so the mines might hold them back long enough to let us get through.'

'That still leaves the problem of the Indos ahead of us,' Alf pointed out.

'Solving half a problem is better than nothing,' Dead-eye informed him. 'We can deal with the ones in front of us a lot easier than we can with the lot coming up on our backsides. So it's one mine each mile, Pete.'

'I'm your man, Sarge.'

They advanced through the swamp at the usual laborious pace, dragging their feet through the mud, pushing the drifting debris aside, swatting the flies and mosquitoes, and being constantly on the alert for sea snakes or the spiders that often dropped off branches when they were brushed. The leeches they could not avoid or combat in any way; they simply had to let them cling there, sucking their blood, until they next stopped to let Pete set another booby-trap with his Claymores. While Pete was doing this, the men burned the countless leeches off themselves with the lit end of a cigarette. However, once Pete had done the same and they were on the move again, more leeches came off the wet leaves to attach themselves to their already ravaged skin. Within half a mile each man would be covered yet again in a mass of slimy leeches, all sucking his blood.

The first Claymore exploded well behind them when they were nearing the end of the swamp. Even from this distance the noise was shocking, a mighty clap of thunder, and when they glanced back they saw a cloud of black smoke boiling up from the area. They even heard men screaming from this distance, but those sounds were much fainter.

Dead-eye grinned at Pete and stuck his thumb in the air. Then they moved off again.

The second Claymore exploded behind them about an hour later. Again, when they glanced backwards, they saw a cloud of black smoke billowing up from the swamp and heard the faint sounds of men screaming. It took little imagination to visualize the devastation caused to the patrols by the explosion, as well as by the dreadful shredding effect of the mine's 350 sharp-edged, red-hot, flying metal slugs.

More concerned for themselves than they were for the enemy, the SAS men moved on, gradually reaching higher ground, where the water only came up to their knees.

Knowing by this that they were almost at the end of the swamp, they stopped for a rest – and to look and listen for the sounds of the enemy. They were lucky to have done so, for they heard the sounds of movement directly ahead, which encouraged them, as usual, to melt into the trees at both sides of the imaginary path, two men to each side, with each man hiding behind his own chosen tree.

Again, a lone soldier emerged from the foliage ahead – a scout out on point – and again Dead-eye slashed his throat with his commando dagger, then lowered his convulsing body into the blood-reddened water.

Knowing that the full patrol would not be far behind, he decided to keep the men where they were and deal with the patrol when it appeared. While they were waiting, the third Claymore exploded behind them, creating another billowing cloud of black smoke and producing more distant screams.

Those booby-traps would ensure that if the Indonesians took any of the SAS troopers alive they would show them no mercy. This merely convinced Dead-eye even more that they should attempt to fight their way out of the swamp, giving no quarter.

Within a few minutes the first members of the patrol emerged from a clear path running through the *belukar* straight ahead. It consisted of ten men.

Dead-eye raised his hand, preparing to give the signal to fire, but did not lower it until the rest of the patrol had emerged from the undergrowth. Meanwhile, Pete Welsh had taken an '80' white-phosphorus incendiary grenade from his webbed belt and was preparing to pull the pin. Alf and Terry were squinting through the sights of their SLRs, but they did not fire when Dead-eye dropped his hand.

Instead, they let Pete throw the grenade. It arced through the air, seeming to travel very slowly – certainly slow enough for one of the enemy to look up, see it coming and shout a warning. That warning came too late. The grenade bounced off a tree right behind the patrol and exploded with a mighty roar, filling the air with silvery-white streams of phosphorus and swirling black smoke, tearing the foliage to shreds, and bowling over two or three of the men. Even as the latter were splashing into the boiling water, Alf and Terry were opening fire with their SLRs, pouring it into the enemy in short, savage bursts that tore them to pieces. Dead-eye and Pete then opened fire as well, firing single shots at selected targets – notably those men who had broken away from the main group and were rushing to take cover behind the trees.

The combined roar of the four SLRs reverberated through the trees, shockingly loud, but could not drown the screams of the men dying and splashing into the swamp. The greenish-brown water was boiling furiously, being kicked up by the hail of bullets, but in less than half a minute it had settled down again, the SAS guns had ceased firing, and ten dead Indonesians were floating and gradually sinking in spreading pools of blood.

'Let's get out of here,' Dead-eye said.

Advancing, they were forced to wade through the blood-reddened water, pushing the drifting, lacerated corpses aside until they had passed through and could enter the same clear path that the enemy had emerged from. They had just done so when an Indonesian helicopter, obviously drawn by the sounds of the fire-fight, flew overhead, hovered above the floating or sinking bodies, then moved on until it was hovering right over Dead-eye and the others.

They froze immediately, glancing up at the helicopter, preparing to fire at it with their SLRs if the actions of the pilot indicated that he had seen them. Obviously knowing that they could not be far away, he flew to and fro over the general area, coming down as low as he dared – so low, in fact, that the slipstream of the rotors was creating a minor hurricane around the hiding men, tearing leaves and branches off the trees. Eventually, however, the pilot gave up and flew off, letting them move on again.

They were just reaching the end of the swamp when the fourth and last Claymore went off behind them, creating the by now customary din and producing more screaming. Elated that the booby-traps had done their job by delaying the advance of the troops behind them, the four men grinned at one another, then waded on. Gradually they came up out of the scum-covered water until it was splashing only around their ankles.

It was just before dusk when they crossed the fire-lane track and Dead-eye decided they should lie up. Slowing down, they turned right, off their route, and moved, continually covering their tracks, into a thick patch of jungle.

Working on the assumption that they were still being followed, Dead-eye left Alf behind as the sentry between their old route and this new hide.

It would be a lonely duty for Alf, but someone had to do it. Once in the hide, with bashas laid out under the trees, Dead-eye gave his report to Terry for transmission to the Haunted House.

As Terry was transmitting, Dead-eye and Pete were diverted by the sounds of distant mortar explosions from an area much further east, which suggested that the Indonesians had gone off in search of them elsewhere.

'Don't believe it for a second,' Dead-eye said. 'That's what the Indos want us to think, but it's just an old trick of theirs. The CTs did the same thing in Malaya: sent some of their men off a good distance to set off some explosions, making you think that's where they were. Then, while you were relaxing, maybe even stopping to rest, thinking the enemy was far away, the main body of men would catch up with you and wipe you off the map. I'd say those mortar explosions are serving the same purpose for the Indos. They want to make us believe they're miles away, but they're right there behind us. That's why Alf is sitting out there on his lonesome: to make sure they don't take us by surprise. We move on at first light.'

They had been out on patrol for little more than a week, but had carried enough rations for two. Therefore, because so much had happened in this single day, and as they were now within a day's march of the border, Dead-eye allowed them to eat as much as they wanted. When they had done so and were settling down, satiated, he ordered them to bury the rations they did not need. This, he explained, would lighten their load on the last leg of the hike. The men did as they were told, then gratefully stretched out on their bashas under the trees.

They slept soundly that night.

16

Rising at first light the following morning, they had a cold breakfast with the last of the rations they had kept, then carefully cleaned up, removing all traces of the hide, and marched back to collect the frozen Alf, who had survived his lonely vigil without incident.

Immensely relieved to be out of the swamp, but still convinced that the Indonesians would not give up the chase until they reached the border, they marched on. The hike took them into the relative ease of primary jungle, though also into a series of high ridges and forested hills, criss-crossed with sparkling streams and deep, dangerous gorges, only some of which had aerial walkways spanning them.

Foiled by a bridgeless gorge not shown on the map, they had to make a detour and found themselves at a location different from the one through which they had entered enemy territory. Here the low hills, with no clear contour lines or outstanding features, made navigation especially difficult. Also, though all of them except Alf had had a decent night's sleep, they were suddenly attacked by the psychological effects of their arduous and brutal flight through the swamp. Alf was edgy and snapped at the others; Pete was slightly disorientated and slow to respond to orders; and Terry, in particular, was showing signs of distress, manifested in his refusal to let anyone else carry the radio, even though he was clearly exhausted.

'I'm the only one who can use it quickly in an emergency,' he said, speaking nonsense. 'And besides, I feel fine.'

The only one not affected appeared to be Dead-eye, though he saw what was happening to the others. Familiar with this syndrome from Malaya, particularly from his experiences in the dreadful Telok Anson swamp, he called more rest periods than normal and gently coaxed the men into eating the high-calorie rations in their escape belts. The chocolate, in particular, would give them back some of the strength they had lost not only through sheer exhaustion, but also by being drained of so much blood by the countless leeches that had fed off them for days.

Just after noon, when the *ulu* was like a steam bath, they saw an enemy soldier in the branches high up a tree, looking directly at them, then signalling frantically with both hands, clearly telling his friends he had seen them. Dead-eye picked off the soldier with a single shot from his SLR, making him spin backwards off the tree and plunge screaming to the ground, smashing through, and snapping off, many branches as he fell. Nevertheless, within minutes, a helicopter was rising from the jungle nearby, from where the soldier had been signalling to. It headed straight towards the SAS men.

'They know where we are,' Dead-eye said. 'That means they'll come after us again. Let's skedaddle as fast as we can.'

Given a positive incentive to keep moving, the men did so, now more alert than they had been in the morning. The helicopter roared overhead, descending vertically, creating a storm, and then hovered directly above them, dangerously close to the trees.

A gunner was kneeling at the side door, taking aim with his Chinese 7.62mm gas-operated machine-gun.

The roar of the gun added to the deafening noise of the helicopter, then the vegetation around the running men went crazy, with palm leaves, thorny branches and splinters of bark exploding from the trees and cascading out in all directions.

'Shit!' Alf exclaimed angrily, his cheek slashed

by a thorny branch, the wound dripping blood. He dropped to one knee beside a screen of bamboo, took aim with his SLR and fired a sustained burst at the helicopter. The gunner fired back, aiming at Alf, who threw himself to one side as a line of bullets ran at him and blew the bamboo screen apart. The flying bamboo cut him even more, making him curse as he rolled away. When he clambered back to his feet, he was bleeding from more cuts to his face, as well as from both hands.

'You look like a pin-cushion,' Pete said, tugging Alf forward. 'Come on! Let's get going.'

The machine-gun was blowing the clearing all to hell as the men melted into the trees beyond it. The pilot, seeing where they had gone, advanced to locate them.

'Fuck this for a lark,' Pete said. He stopped, tugged an '80' grenade from his belt, pulled the pin, then swung his arm and hurled the grenade as hard as he could, on a very high arc. It exploded like a thunderclap in front of the chopper, filling the air with streaming silvery-white phosphorus and billowing smoke. Though it did not damage the helicopter, it either shocked or temporarily blinded the pilot, making him briefly lose control.

The chopper tilted violently sideways, its nose inching through the cloud of phosphorus and smoke, its rotors, which had been spinning close to the trees, now actually hitting them. First they chopped off branches, then they buckled badly, and finally one of them broke off completely and fell to the ground. Crippled, the helicopter leaned sideways and plunged to earth, smashing down through the branches, bringing whole trees down with it, and then exploding into a fierce ball of yellow-and-blue fire that engulfed the surrounding trees and foliage, creating an even bigger blaze.

Pete raised his right fist and shook it, grinning like a loon, then he and the others hurried away from the inferno before the smoke choked them.

Infuriated, the Indonesians redoubled their efforts to either destroy or capture the SAS patrol. Shortly after another helicopter had skimmed over the jungle canopy, staying well out of gunshot range and merely tracking those below, relaying their position to the soldiers on the ground, enemy mortars started firing repeatedly. The explosions erupted all around the fleeing SAS men, showering them with soil and vegetation, but not actually hitting them. While the explosions continued, the enemy troops advanced faster than ever, zigzagging from one tree to the other and gradually catching up.

Not willing to call for a helicopter lift while they were on the Indonesian side of the border and the enemy were so close, but determined to protect the radio at all costs, Dead-eye urged the patrol on while he took up the rear and picked off the soldiers as they appeared. One went down, then another, a third and a fourth. Temporarily foiled, the remainder stopped advancing and took cover behind the trees, only reappearing long enough to fire short bursts at Dead-eye, where he was kneeling behind a bamboo screen.

One of the Indonesians climbed up a tree to try and locate Dead-eye's precise position. Dead-eye accounted for him with a single shot and the man spun off the branch and plunged screaming to the jungle floor, smashing through branches and kicking up a cloud of soil and mud when he thumped into the ground. Another started climbing and was also picked off, likewise crashing down through the trees.

Seeing the futility of what they were doing, the Indonesians remained in hiding, but unleashed a concentrated barrage of mortar shells on the general vicinity as determined by the sound of Dead-eye's gunfire. They were not too far off. The forest around Dead-eye became a hell of exploding earth and foliage, with trees set on fire and the smoke gradually swirling around Dead-eye.

Choking, he jumped up and ran, following the rest of the patrol. Seeing him, the Indonesians released a fusillade of fire that had bullets whipping past his head and blowing lumps of bark off the trees. He dropped low, turned around, fired a short burst, then jumped up and ran again, repeating this time and again until he was within sight of the patrol.

As Dead-eye approached, Pete and Alf knelt facing him, shielding Terry and the radio, and laid down a fusillade of fire that forced the enemy to take cover again. When Dead-eye reached them, he saw Terry standing nervously at an aerial walkway that spanned a deep gorge. Looking down, momentarily dizzy, Dead-eye saw a river squeezing through a bottle-neck of large rocks and emerging at the other side, directly below the walkway, as a raging torrent.

'Christ!' he whispered involuntarily.

'My knees are shaking, boss,' Terry said, wiping sweat from his face. 'I don't think I can cross this.'

'You have to. We all have to.'

'It makes me dizzy just to look down.'

'Don't look down. Look straight ahead. Keep your eyes fixed on the jungle at the other side and pretend you're on solid ground. Do it now, lad. Don't hesitate.'

Terry wiped sweat from his face, took a deep breath, stepped forward and then stopped again.

'I can't!'

'Yes, you can.' Dead-eye pushed him gently, but

Terry still would not move. Only when bullets started whipping around them did he step onto the walkway, taking one tentative step, then stopping again to grab the horizontal bamboo railing on his right, the other hand being engaged with his SLR.

This simple movement caused Terry to glance sideways, probably to check that he was really holding the railing; but then his gaze took in the wide spaces between the uprights, the fragile look of the bamboo walkway, and the raging torrent that wound between the rocky walls of the gorge a good 100 feet down.

Terry started sweating and shaking. Clearly, he was more frightened at being on the swaying walkway than he was of the bullets still whistling about him. Pete and Alf, meanwhile, were still facing the Indonesians, keeping them pinned down as much as possible with short bursts of fire.

'Get moving, Terry,' Dead-eye said.

'This bridge is moving, boss!'

'It moves, but it's not about to break apart. It's just the way they're built, Terry. Start walking. Don't look down.'

'I can't move, boss. I'm sorry.'

Dead-eye turned around and saw the enemy in the *ulu*, either lying in the tall grass and only jumping up to get off a quick shot or sticking their heads out from behind the trees for the same reason. Pete and Alf were still kneeling by the walkway, their SLRs roaring in turn as they kept the Indonesians pinned down.

'I'm going to take Terry over the walkway,' Dead-eye told them. 'Try to keep those bastards back until we get to the other side. When we do, I'll give you covering fire until you get across.'

'Right, boss,' Pete said.

Dead-eye stepped onto the walkway. As soon as he did so, it moved, swaying a little from left to right. It was being shaken constantly by the wind sweeping through the gorge, but it swayed more with each move Dead-eye took, which made it seem very dangerous.

Dead-eye grabbed the bamboo support on his right. Looking down, he felt dizzy. The walkway itself was only the width of its three lengths of thick bamboo, laid down side by side and strapped together with rattan. It was hardly much wider than two human feet placed close together. The uprights angled out and in again overhead, bending where they were strapped with rattan to the horizontal holds.

You could slide your hand along the holds only as far as the next upright. Once there, you had to remove your hand for a moment and lift it over the upright before grabbing the horizontal hold again.

That was what had done Terry in, Dead-eye

realized. He had automatically looked down when he took hold of the upright and now he was afraid to let go and move further along.

Knowing this, Dead-eye carefully made his way forward, along the narrow, swaying, creaking walkway, until he was standing right behind Terry. He slung his SLR over his shoulder, then placed his free hand on Terry's elbow, holding him steady.

'Start walking,' he said. When Terry did not move immediately, apart from visibly shaking, Dead-eye pushed him forward gently, but insistently, by the elbow and he took his first step. 'That's it,' Dead-eye said in a soft, mesmeric tone of voice. 'Easy does it. Don't look down. Keep your eyes on the trees straight ahead. It's not too far to walk.'

In fact, the walkway was about 150 feet in length, though being so narrow it looked a lot longer. Its swaying was visible, its creaking constant, and the wind blowing along the gorge had the force of a hammer blow.

Given the wide spaces between the uprights, Dead-eye realized, a man could be blown off the walkway with nothing to stop him falling to his doom. Terry must have been aware of this fact, also, but prompted by Dead-eye, he did at least keep going forward, only hesitating when he had to let go of the horizontal bamboo and stand unsupported for the second it took to lift his hand over the upright and take hold again.

Those moments always seemed like an eternity, but they had to be braved.

'That's it,' Dead-eye said. 'Good.'

They were about halfway across when the walkway, already swaying noisily, shook suddenly and swayed even more.

When Terry's knuckles whitened over the bamboo, displaying his panic, Dead-eye glanced backwards and saw that Alf had jumped onto the walkway. Amazingly, Alf was moving backwards, holding the horizontal bamboo with one hand and firing short bursts from his SLR with the other, keeping the barrel steady by pressing the stock into his hip. Alf was giving covering fire to Pete as he, in turn, did the same for Terry and Dead-eye. Pete was still kneeling in the tall grass near the edge of the gorge, firing his SLR, reloading, firing again, and occasionally jumping up to hurl a hand-grenade. The explosions tore the shrubbery apart and obscured the advancing soldiers behind veils of white-phosphorus dust and smoke.

'It's only Alf,' Dead-eye explained to reassure Terry. 'He's jumped onto the walkway. Keep going. You're over halfway. You'll soon be on the other side. Take it slow and steady.'

Understandably, Terry was feeling more tension

because he was also humping the radio on top of his heavy bergen. This made his balance more precarious when the walkway swayed from side to side, as it was now doing more than ever as Alf backed across it.

At that moment, the enemy started firing their mortars at the walkway. The first explosion erupted near Pete, almost bowling him sideways and certainly covering him in showering soil and foliage. The second shell looped down past the walkway and exploded against the side of the gorge just below it, hurling rocks and soil into the rapids far below.

The walkway shook violently again. This time, when Dead-eye glanced back, he saw that Pete had also jumped onto it and was, like Alf, moving backwards while firing his SLR at the troops advancing out of the undergrowth.

'Faster!' Dead-eye snapped at Terry, wanting to leave the walkway free for the other two. 'Damn it, Terry, get going!'

Impelled by the urgency in Dead-eye's voice, Terry gathered his courage and practically ran the rest of the way across, jumping gratefully onto the solid ground at the far side. Even as Dead-eye followed him, Terry was turning around and unslinging his SLR to give covering fire to Alf and Pete. He had already opened fire as Dead-eye jumped onto the ground and also turned back to add to their fire.

Two more mortar shells exploded on the far bank, dangerously close to the pinions of the walkway. A third shell looped down over the walkway, narrowly missed the bamboo uprights, and continued down into the gorge, exploding in the rapids and creating a great mushroom of boiling water.

Alf was, by now, halfway across, still moving backwards and firing at the same time. Pete had just commenced his own, painfully slow, backwards crossing while firing short but effective bursts at the soldiers who were emerging from the *ulu*. Hit by Pete's bullets, but only wounded, one of the Indonesians fell, rolled off the edge and plunged screaming down into the rapids. Others convulsed and fell along the grassy, irregular edge of the gorge. More emerged from the *ulu* and risked Pete's bullets to try and reach the end of the walkway. Some finally made it.

Running out of time and now protected a little by the covering fire of Dead-eye and Terry, Alf turned around and hurried towards them. By the time he left the walkway, jumping onto the solid ground beside the other two, Pete was halfway across, though still walking backwards and firing at the same time.

Four enemy soldiers started onto the bridge, but were cut down by the combined fire-power of Dead-eye, Terry and Alf. The soldiers crumpled in a heap, one practically on top of the other, effectively blocking access to the walkway. Seeing this, the other soldiers retreated back behind the trees along the edge of the gorge and fired a sustained fusillade at Pete, who was now just over halfway across. The hail of bullets tore the bamboo uprights and horizontals apart, with pieces of bamboo sailing down into the rapids and sharp splinters showering over Pete.

'*Run!*' Dead-eye bawled.

Pete was turning around to do just that when he jerked epileptically, dropped his SLR, and fell chest-first against a horizontal length of bamboo. Hanging there for a second, he watched his rifle fall down into the rapids, then he straightened up again, holding his left arm, and staggered on across the bridge toward his comrades. His arm was a bloody mess, with blood spurting out of punctured veins and dropping like rain into the gorge.

'Jesus!' Alf whispered, then fired a savage burst across the gorge, hoping to hit one of the many soldiers hiding behind the trees at the other side. He did little good. More bullets were punching into Pete, making him jerk and quiver and almost fall over toward the spaces between the uprights.

A machine-gunner, also well hidden in the trees, started firing at the spot where the walkway was fixed to the side of the gorge. He was trying to blow it apart.

'Faster!' Dead-eye bawled at the now badly wounded, bloody and staggering Pete. 'Faster, damn it! *Faster!*'

But Pete could go no faster. He was losing blood too rapidly. He managed to remain upright, holding onto the handrail, but he was swaying dangerously from side to side and jerking spasmodically as more bullets punched into him – even as the hail of bullets from the machine-gun was blowing asunder the supports at the side of the gorge.

'Come on, Pete!' Alf screamed, then fired another angry burst across the gorge.

But Pete fell on his hands and knees in the middle of the walkway, looking straight down that dizzying drop as his blood squirted out from the bullet holes in his body and shattered arm to rain down on the rapids.

Alf dropped his SLR and nearly jumped onto the walkway, intent on rescuing his friend, but Dead-eye grabbed him by the shoulders and jerked him back, practically slamming him face-down into the dirt. 'No, Alf! It's too late!'

As Alf sat up again, the supports savaged by the

machine-gun finally came away from the gorge wall and the whole walkway started breaking up, with great lengths of bamboo sailing down into the gorge. The rest of the fragile construction soon followed, breaking up like the pieces of a gigantic jigsaw puzzle. The three lengths of bamboo that had formed the actual walkway were the last to break apart, with the separate pieces slipping out of their rattan ties and falling into the rapids far below.

Still fixed to the side of the gorge where Deadeye, Terry and Alf were kneeling, the remaining half of the walkway started tilting down, tearing away from the rocks in which it had been embedded, then breaking up even as Pete, still on his hands and knees, slid backwards to the broken end, wrapped his arms around a crossbeam, then found himself hanging from it with his legs kicking frantically in mid-air.

He did not hang there long. The pain from his wounded arm made him scream and let go. A final burst from the machine-gun tore him away for good and he fell, screaming louder, tumbling like a wind-blown leaf, to the bottom of the gorge, where he splashed into the raging rapids, was smashed against the rocks, and then was swept away out of sight to a watery grave.

'*Bastards!*' Alf screamed. He stood up to fire his

SLR at the soldiers over the gorge, but Dead-eye jerked him back down, pushed him towards the trees, and bawled, 'Go! They can't get at us now. Let's get the hell out of here!'

The three men picked themselves up and hurried into the trees, away from a final, frustrated volley of fire from the other side of the gorge.

They had made it back.

Late that afternoon, when they had crossed the border and Dead-eye was certain that the Indonesians would not pursue them by helicopter, he told Terry to radio for one of their own choppers, asking the pilot to home in on the SARBE beacon and fix their position relative to the LZ. The message transmitted back was that the pilot was going to do more than that: he was going to save them from the long hike to the RV by picking them up.

While they waited for the chopper to arrive, the distraught Terry and, particularly, Alf, finished off the last of the high-calorie rations in their escape belts, then distracted themselves by cleaning and oiling their much-used weapons. Meanwhile, Dead-eye kept himself busy by making the last entries in his notebook, detailing everything about the mission for later analysis by the 'green slime', the officers of SAS intelligence.

Forty minutes later, a Wessex Mark 1 helicopter

arrived overhead, making a lot of noise and whipping up the foliage when it hovered just above the treetops, about 90 feet up. Unable to land, the pilot had his crewman lower his winch wire with two harnesses attached. The harnesses fell down through the trees, bouncing off the branches, and finally dangled, bobbing up and down, a few inches above their heads.

The three men piled their bergens into one of the winches, Terry took the second, and the wires were then rapidly reeled in. Alf went up next. Finally, Dead-eye was pulled up and scrambled gratefully into the chopper, which was piloted by his old sparring partner Army Air Corps Lieutenant Ralph Ellis.

'Had a nice ten day's jaunt in the countryside, did you?' he asked.

'Very nice, thanks,' Dead-eye replied deadpan. '*You* should try it some time.'

The helicopter ascended towards the crimson sun, then turned north and flew above the jungle canopy, heading for Kuching. By nightfall the men were being debriefed in the Haunted House.

The mission was over.

17

Sergeant Richard Parker, Corporal Alf Laughton and Trooper Terry Malkin were returned with the rest of D Squadron to the SAS base in Hereford, but the war in Borneo did not end with their departure.

Following their successful patrol to the bend in the River Koemba, other patrols retraced their route and photographed the fire-track they had crossed. Further 'Claret' raids were mounted a few months later and, greatly aided by the intelligence brought back by Dead-eye's team, were even more successful.

D Squadron was replaced by the returning A Squadron, led by Major Peter de la Billière, who would eventually become the commander of the SAS. Under his brilliant leadership, A Squadron forged a closer relationship with the border battalions, made great improvements in the organization for supplying patrols in the field, and worked closely with the 1st/2nd Gurkhas in a series of highly successful cross-border operations. These included intelligence-gathering forays west and south of Stass; tapping Indonesian telephone lines 10 miles inside enemy territory, which produced invaluable taped conversations between various high-ranking Indonesian Army officers; snatching top-secret documents from an Indonesian Army building; and laying minefields in Sabah's formerly unexplored jungles.

Plans were being drawn up for even more ambitious 'Claret' raids when, in March 1966, a military government replaced the aggressive President Sukarno and the war eased a little. The war ceased completely when a treaty was concluded between Indonesia and Malaya the following August. This brought to a definite end the 'undeclared' war that had lasted nearly four years, killing 114 Commonwealth soldiers, including Corporal Pete Welsh and six other SAS men. The Indonesians suffered five times that number of casualties.

The so-called 'Confrontation' in Borneo had shown the necessity of having troops who could solve the unique problems raised by an 'undeclared' war where British forces could not overtly take the fight into enemy territory. It also confirmed once and for all that the kind of hearts-and-minds campaign devised by the SAS in Malaya could work wonders where direct military action was not a viable option.

As with every SAS campaign, the men who took part in the Confrontation in Borneo were affected by it in different ways.

The 'newcomer', Terry Malkin, returning from Borneo as a toughened, experienced trooper, was sent almost immediately to take part in the counter-insurgency campaign in Aden. There he became one of that legendary group of men who, disguised as Arabs, infiltrated the souks and bazaars to assassinate leading members of the National Liberation Front by use of the 'double tap' – firing a 9mm Browning High Power handgun at close range – as part of the daring 'Keeni Meeni' operations.

Corporal Alf Laughton, who had survived the horrors of the Telok Anson swamp in Malaya approximately five years before his Borneo experience, was deeply shocked by the loss of his best friend, Pete Welsh, and emotionally drained by his two gruelling campaigns. At his own request he was sent for treatment to 'the thinking man's Belsen' – Ward 11 of the British Army Psychiatric Unit – where he was gradually coaxed out of his depression and returned to the regiment to become a ruthlessly efficient member of the Directing Staff at 22 SAS Training Wing, Hereford.

Like Corporal Laughton, Sergeant Richard Parker

had physically survived the horrors of both jungle campaigns, but was psychologically scarred by his experiences, as well as by the loss of so many good friends. Eschewing psychiatric help, Dead-eye solved his problems in his own way, mainly by spending most of his spare time alone, reading books on military theory, and by training himself to live without the need for friends who might be killed in battle. In 1972, by then dubbed 'Soldier C' by some snooping journalists, he was one of those who took part in the fight to clear the fanatical Adoo guerrillas from the summit of the mighty Jebel Dhofar in Oman. He survived that as well.

'Tell me in one sentence,' Terry Malkin said in the Paludrine Club in the SAS base at Hereford, just before they were shipped out to Aden, 'how you've managed to survive all that shit.'

'Who dares wins,' Dead-eye told him.

OTHER BOOKS IN THIS SERIES

Available now at newsagents and booksellers

SOLDIER A SAS: Behind Iraqi Lines	£4.99 net
SOLDIER B SAS: Heroes of the South Atlantic	£4.99 net
SOLDIER C SAS: Secret War in Arabia	£4.99 net
SOLDIER D SAS: The Colombian Cocaine War	£4.99 net
SOLDIER E SAS: Sniper Fire in Belfast	£4.99 net
SOLDIER F SAS: Guerrillas in the Jungle	£4.99 net
SOLDIER G SAS: The Desert Raiders	£4.99 net